BROADBAND LAN TECHNOLOGY

The Artech House Telecommunication Library

Preparing and Delivering Effective Technical Presentations by David L. Adamy

The Executive Guide to Video Teleconferencing by Ronald J. Bohm and Lee B. Templeton

The Telecommunications Deregulation Sourcebook, Stuart N. Brotman, ed.

Digital Cellular Radio by George Calhoun

E-Mail Stephen A. Caswell

The ITU in a Changing World by George A. Codding, Jr. and Anthony M. Rutkowski

Design and Prospects for the ISDN by G. DICENET

Communications by Manus Egan

Introduction to Satellite Communication by Bruce R. Elbert

Television Programming across National Boundaries: The EBU and OIRT Experience by Ernest Eugster

The Competition for Markets in International Telecommunications by Ronald S. Eward

A Bibliography of Telecommunications and Socio-Economic Development by Heather E. Hudson

New Directions in Satellite Communications: Challenges for North and South, Heather E. Hudson, ed.

Communication Satellites in the Geostationary Orbit by Donald M. Jansky and Michel C. Jeruchim

World Atlas of Satellites, Donald M. Jansky, ed.

Handbook of Satellite Telecommunications and Broadcasting, L. Ya. Kantor, ed.

World-Traded Services: The Challenge for the Eighties by Raymond J. Krommenacker

Telecommunications: An Interdisciplinary Text, Leonard Lewin, ed.
Telecommunications in the U.S.: Trends and Policies, Leonard Lewin, ed.
Introduction to Telecommunication Electronics by A. Michael Noll
Teleconferencing Technology and Applications by Christine H. Olgren and Lorne A. Parker
The ISDN Workshop: INTUG Proceedings, G. Russell Pipe, ed.
Integrated Services Digital Networks by Anthony M. Rutkowski
Writing and Managing Winning Technical Proposals by Timothy Whalen
The Law and Regulation of International Space Communication by Harold M. White, Jr. and Rita Lauria White

BROADBAND
LAN
TECHNOLOGY

Gary Y. Kim
Artech House

Library of Congress Cataloging-in-Publication Data

Kim, Gary Y.
  Broadband LAN technology.

  Includes index.
  1. Local area networks (Computer networks)
2. Broadband communication systems. I. Title.
TK5105.5.K55   1988   004.6'8   88-24232
ISBN   0-89006-291-9

International Standard Book Number: 0-89006-291-9
Library of Congress Catalog Card Number: 88-24232

10   9   8   7   6   5   4   3   2   1

Contents

Preface

This book was written for data-communication professionals seeking better knowledge of broadband technology. It focuses heavily on the physical-layer hardware users will encounter when designing, installing, or maintaining a broadband facility. It was written this way to meet an important information need that has arisen as cable television (CATV) technology has found greater acceptance as a local area network medium.

Initially used in terminal-host environments, military and scientific settings, LANs based on broadband physical media became more popular during the late 1980s as demand for bandwidth and facility-wide connectivity grew. Spurred by interest in the Manufacturing Automation Protocol and the proliferation of personal computers, many system integrators, LAN vendors, and computer manufacturers began to offer broadband as well as baseband networks for their customers.

Although well versed in digital technology, many end-users and suppliers found they had little knowledge of CATV principles and techniques. The mirror image was that most engineers and technical personnel who had grown up with the cable TV industry had little knowledge of the computer environment and data-communication networks.

This book hopes to make a contribution by demystifying broadband technology for data communication, management information system, information system, computer center, PC specialist, and other communication professionals.

What I know about broadband I owe primarily to countless old hands in the CATV business, most of whom are vice presidents or directors of engineering at leading firms in the business. Their guidance and patient explanations have been invaluable. Through them I have come to love an industry that feels more like a large, extended family than a multibillion-dollar media giant.

If there are any mistakes in my explanations I take full responsibility for them. My teachers have been patient. I hope their student has learned his lessons well. Readers may contact me for clarification or for further \information at International Thomson Communications, Denver, Colorado, publisher of *CED,* a monthly technical journal devoted to information on broadband and other network technologies. We may be able to help readers find resources to answer questions and solve problems.

I now know why authors thank their families in prefaces to books. It is a solitary endeavor based on time stolen from one's children and spouse. Without their sacrifice this book would not exist, and I thank them gratefully.

Gary Kim
August 1988

Chapter 1
Local Area Networks: An Introduction

Local area networks (LANs)—privately owned communication networks linking computers and other devices in a single building or multi-building complexes—are in the news these days and will become increasingly important in the next several years as more personal computers (PCs) and intelligent devices of all kinds appear in offices and factories, at colleges and universities, hospitals, military installations, and governmental agencies.

LANs originally became popular as a way to connect high-end workstations in terminal-to-host environments. Later, they also became popular as a way to share expensive peripheral devices, such as printers and data storage devices, among many PC users. Today, access to data bases—especially distributed data bases—is also becoming more important. In some ways, LANs resemble the traditional computer systems commonly found in many offices and factories with a central computer wired to many terminals scattered throughout an office or plant. These terminals normally are input-output devices only and have no stand-alone intelligence or processing power. Terminals can communicate with each other only through the central processor. This type of network is called a *centralized network*.

Like these centralized terminal-host systems, LANs run cabling between devices, but the devices connected can be intelligent (such as PCs), rather than simply terminals. Unlike terminal-host systems, the devices communicate directly with each other, rather than simply through the central computer. Each terminal also has its own processor and is capable of functioning independently of other devices on the network. In short, a LAN connects many independent and intelligent devices. LANs typically are used to connect heterogeneous devices such as printers, disk drives, PCs, process or numerical controllers, minicomputers or main-frame computers, scanners, and robots. LANs use a form of *distributed processing* rather than centralized processing.

Nevertheless, some LANs are used to link terminals and hosts, and others use microcomputers as terminals to access host computers. LANs also differ from more traditional multiprocessing systems, which also have distributed processing nodes. Multiprocessor systems are coupled much more tightly than most LANs are, and multiprocessors usually place greater reliance on shared memory, centralized control, and completely integrated communications. LANs normally allow completely localized processing and memory. Broadband networks, in particular, allow heterogeneous use. It is possible, for example, to run several distinct networks over a single cable and to run telemetry or security systems (security cameras, energy monitoring devices, or temperature- and humidity-sensing devices) in addition to the various data communication systems. Also, broadband operation allows simultaneous transmission of multiple channels of video and hundreds of channels of data.

This section is a brief tutorial on LANs as a backdrop to a fuller discussion of broadband LANs. (See Fig. 1.1.) LANs differ from other types of communication systems by geographic area of coverage (size), ownership, data transmission and error rates, government regulation, and to a certain extent the type of information that is transmitted.

One way to describe a LAN as a communication system is to separate it from existing wide area and metropolitan area networks. Think of the long-distance telephone system and satellite systems as *wide area networks* (WANs). WANs are simply networks that span a large distance. Think of your local cable television (CATV) system or local phone company as a *metropolitan area network* (MAN). The MAN covers a much smaller geographic area such as a single city. Think of a network linking employees in a single company or on a single campus as a local area network. As the name implies, a LAN is a communication network covering only a small ("local") area.

Ownership is another way to separate LANs from WANs and MANs. WANs and MANs are not owned by the actual end-users. Instead, customers contract for telephone or CATV services, for example. LANs, on the other hand, are almost always privately owned, the exception being educational and governmental LANs (public universities, military installations, government agencies). AT&T, MCI, and Sprint own their transmission facilities, and customers pay to use them. US West, Ameritech, Tele-Communications, Inc., and American Television and Communications also own their networks, and customers subscribe to CATV and local telephone companies.

Unlike CATV systems, local telephone networks and long-distance communication networks, which are regulated in certain ways by the Federal Communications Commission (FCC), LANs are not subject to federal

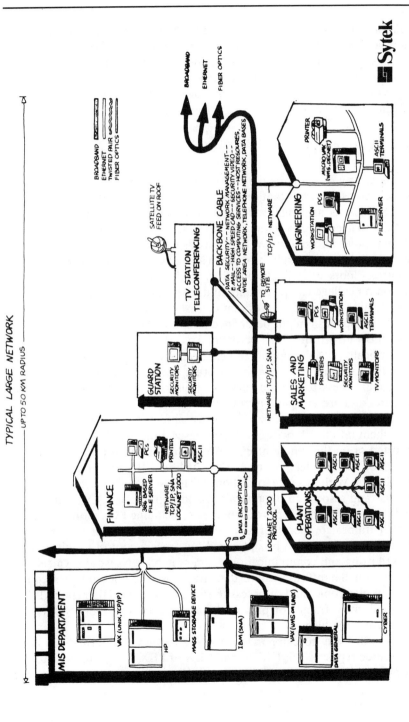

Figure 1.1 Enterprise networks connect all users or devices at a single company site or sites. (Courtesy of Sytek.)

regulatory jurisdiction. A LAN user typically owns the entire transmission system and all the devices on that system: network controllers and monitors, interfaces, modems, cabling, wallplates, data storage devices, printers, PCs, amplifiers or repeaters, terminals, minicomputers, and mainframe computers. The LAN user also owns (under license) the software that runs on the network.

1.1 LANs DEFINED

As a way of demarcating them from WANs and MANs, LANs are also defined as a system that processes data at high speeds with low error rates. So, LANs are usually defined as privately owned communication networks that connect a variety of devices over relatively small distances and that move information at high speeds with low error rates. A "relatively small distance" might be defined as a single floor on a single building or several floors of a single building. LANs are becoming increasingly common on college campuses and military bases in addition to industrial, commercial, and scientific sites that consist of many buildings.

"High speeds" might be defined as speeds between 0.1 Mb/s and 30 Mb/s. "Low error rates" can be defined as ranging from 10^{-8} or 10^{-11}.

Typically, LANs support full connectivity: every device should have the ability to communicate with any other device on the network. LANs offer equal access to the network by all users, are relatively easy to reconfigure, and are available at relatively low cost.

LANs can be categorized in many different ways. One way is to divide them into five types of networks based either on the type of devices supported or on the function: PC LANs, general-purpose LANs, factory-automation LANs, data-switch LANs (such as CBX or PBX), and high-speed LANs. With this categorization, PC LANs would be used to connect only PCs and associated peripherals. General-purpose LANs would have the ability to link many types of processors, including PCs, minicomputers, or main frames, or peripherals associated with those devices. Factory-automation LANs would be optimized for process control requiring real-time reporting and communication. Data-switch LANs would typically be found in smaller offices, where data traffic is sporadic and files consist mostly of electronic mail or access to small data bases. High-speed LANs would link main frames or provide *backbone* access to subnetworks that must move large files.

Another way to categorize a LAN is to view the network as being one of three types: LAN, HSLN, and CBX or PBX. Very high speed local networks, such as those traditionally used in computer rooms to connect main frames and mass storage units over very short distances, generally are not used for networking minicomputers, microcomputers, and other less expensive peripherals. Often known as *high-speed local networks* (HSLNs), these systems normally transmit at about 50 Mb/s to a relatively limited number of devices.

The *computerized branch exchange* (CBX) or *private branch exchange* (PBX) is a digital switching system that can handle both voice and data. CBX data rates are typically low (about 64 kb/s); they may be appropriate where infrequent and small data files need to be moved between terminals or between terminals and a host computer, or where rewiring is not possible and terminals and phones are collocated. LANs and HSLNs use *packet switching* (whereby messages are switched to addressed terminals), while CBX networks use *circuit switching*.

Yet another way to view LANs is to divide them into three basic categories based on size. *Work-group LANs* would consist mostly of PC networks connecting several microcomputers and peripherals. *Departmental LANs* might combine PC communication and terminal-to-host communication with minicomputers. A departmental LAN might also be perceived as linking more users than would a work group—scores of users rather than a few. *Enterprise LANs* might be perceived as connecting local users and all devices at a single facility (all terminals, processors, and PCs of a university, military base, or hospital, for example). Enterprise networks might also be considered as connecting every user at a single enterprise at each branch site. An example might be a single network spanning the branch offices of a major financial services firm located throughout the continental United States.

1.1.1 Topology

LAN architecture can be divided into star, ring, bus, and tree networks, based on the physical layout of the cabling running to nodes or stations on the network. (See Fig. 1.2.) The PBX, for example, is a star: all nodes are direct-wired to a central control point. Communications between stations on a star network must pass through the central controller for routing to the receiving station, and all messages are switched over physically discrete paths. Star networks set up direct connections between communicating stations through the central controller. Once the connection is established, the stations communicate as though they were connected point-to-point.

Ring and bus networks, by contrast, broadcast their messages: each station on the network is passed by any single communication between

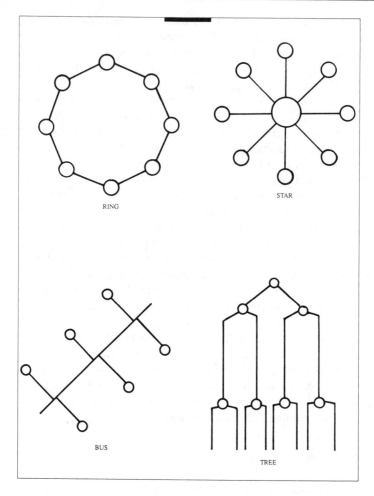

Figure 1.2 Network topologies.

any two stations. On ring networks all nodes are linked serially in a closed loop, and all transmitted signals must travel through each station on their way to the receiving station. Rings can operate *unidirectionally* (transmitting only in a single direction) or *bidirectionally* (transmitting in either direction); in either case, each station repeats messages received if it is not the receiving station.

On a simple bus network all transmissions are broadcast to all other stations on the network, and all nodes are connected to a single length of cable. Ethernet and IEEE 802.3 networks are simple bus networks.

A broadband network is a type of complex bus network resembling a tree because it is structured with a common point of communication called a *headend*, with all nodes branching off trunk and feeder cables that radiate from the headend. On a single-cable broadband network, signals return to a common headend on one set of frequencies and travel outbound from the common headend on a separate set of frequencies. On dual-cable networks a single cable is used for outbound signals, and a separate cable is used for return signals.

Broadband network topology is a tree. However, broadband LAN logic acts like a ring or bus. The token bus network, IEEE 802.4 manufacturing automation protocol (MAP), for example, is physically structured as a tree. Messages pass between stations sequentially, however, just as if the network were a physical ring. The logic of contention broadband networks, based on a contention access method, known as *carrier sense multiple access with collision detection* (CSMA/CD), acts just like a simple bus network.

Ethernet was one of the earliest bus systems in widespread use, utilizing both baseband and broadband signaling. Hyperchannel, one of the oldest high-speed networks, also uses the baseband bus architecture. Because multiple devices share a common transmission path, only one device can transmit at any time without interference occurring. So a key problem in any bus network is to control the transmission. On a single point-to-point link this is a relatively simple matter. If the line is *full-duplex*, allowing both stations to transmit simultaneously, there is no problem at all. If the line is *half-duplex*, allowing only a single station to transmit at a given time, a simple method for taking turns is possible. In more complex systems, *polling* is an option. (See Fig. 1.3.) In polling systems a master station sequentially addresses each station on the network. The master station can either download information to a remote station (possibly passing on a message from a previously polled station) or ask whether the station has any messages to transmit. If message lengths are typically small and real-time communication is not essential, many stations can be supported.

An important distinction here is that digital signaling methods, such as Ethernet, are half-duplex, whereas analog signaling methods, such as CSMA/CD broadband, are full-duplex.

Another important consideration for bus networks is the signal level at which transmissions are made. Levels must be high enough to overcome any transmission losses between the end devices but low enough to avoid overloading the receiver. That requirement is not too difficult in a point-to-point application. However, it is tougher in a larger network because

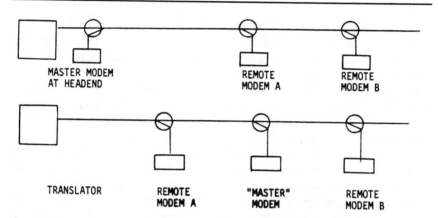

Figure 1.3 In a polling network, a master modem interrogates stations in turn. (Courtesy of Halley Systems, Inc.)

of the sheer number of devices and the corresponding increase in possible signal level variations between any two stations on the network. The problem is made more manageable by the use of repeaters or amplifiers, which essentially break a large network up into a series of smaller network segments. Transmission levels then can be adjusted by each of the amplification stages to the prescribed network signal level.

A bus network using a baseband signaling system is digital. Only a single signal occupies the transmission path at a single time. Signals propagate bidirectionally on the medium at distances up to a few kilometers without the use of special repeating segments. A 50-Ω coaxial cable or twisted pair wire is usually used for a baseband system, and transmission speeds can be as high as 10 Mb/s for Ethernet systems. The maximum number of taps on a single Ethernet LAN ranges from 30 to 100, and the maximum distance between any two stations is set at a precise multiple of 2.5 m to avoid reflections. Repeaters can be used to link two or more Ethernet subnetworks.

Bus networks can also use broadband signaling methods. Broadband signaling is analog and uses *frequency division multiplexing* (FDM) to run multiple channels and multiple signals on the medium at any given moment. Propagation of signals is unidirectional, and distances spanned can be less than a mile to tens of miles. Broadband systems using 75-Ω coaxial cable are based on principles and equipment borrowed from the CATV industry. (See Fig. 1.4.) With the advent of the MAP, however, a single-channel and fixed-frequency version of broadband called *carrier band* or *single-channel broadband* has developed. Used for subnetworking on broadband

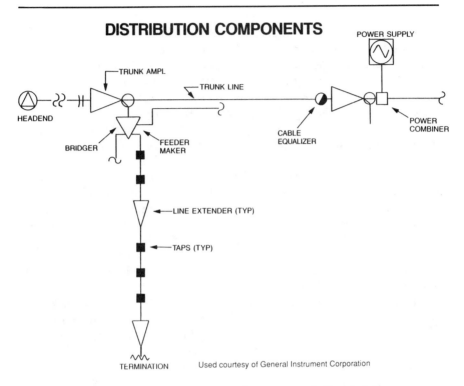

DISTRIBUTION COMPONENTS

POWER SUPPLY

TRUNK AMPL

TRUNK LINE

HEADEND

BRIDGER

FEEDER MAKER

CABLE EQUALIZER

POWER COMBINER

LINE EXTENDER (TYP)

TAPS (TYP)

TERMINATION   Used courtesy of General Instrument Corporation

Figure 1.4 Distribution components. (Courtesy of General Instrument Corporation.)

backbone networks, carrier band uses bidirectional propagation, a fixed transmission frequency, and no amplifiers (or, at least, none are recommended).

Ring networks basically consist of a serial chain of repeater stations, each of which repeats and regenerates the signals it receives. Each repeater station also serves as a device attachment site. Because each device attachment point also serves as a repeater site, a ring network can span longer distances than a baseband bus network can. Also, since a ring is basically a collection of simple point-to-point links operating unidirectionally, the electronics, fault location, and maintenance issues are simpler than for bus networks. On the other hand, some problems are inherent in a ring topology. A cable break anywhere on the ring breaks down the whole network. If any repeater station fails, the whole network breaks down. Preventing timing problems, providing methods for new station addition, removal, and access token regeneration are other important tasks.

None of the aforementioned problems are insurmountable, and many can be solved by the use of a hybrid topology. This popular variant of the ring architecture is the *star-ring*, sometimes called a *ring of stars*. The star-ring uses wiring concentrators. The cable physically loops back into the wiring concentrator between each repeater-node segment, which facilitates fault isolation and new node attachment. Because the cable passes into and out of the wiring concentrator after each repeater station, it is possible to install bypass switches that can route signals around any failed repeater station, thus preserving ring integrity.

On larger ring networks a bridge concept can be used to break up the system into smaller segments. The full network consists of a series of wire concentrator networks linked by one or more bridges. In essence, there is a backbone ring linked by bridges. Each bridge might have one or more connections to a distinct subnetwork of wiring concentrator loops. This concept has several advantages: (1) Timing is easier because the signals are synchronized at each bridge site. (2) Cable failure at subnetwork will not cause the full network to crash. (3) A bridged network is more efficient when heavy traffic is confined to each subnetwork. The backbone ring capacity is reserved solely for messages that must flow from stations on one subnetwork to stations on another subnetwork. Intranetwork traffic is confined to the subnetwork level.

1.1.2 LAN Media

In many cases, there is a relationship between a LAN's architecture, or topology, and its medium. Twisted pair wire can be configured as a bus, ring, or star, but not as a tree. Generally speaking, baseband coaxial cable can be configured as a bus or ring, but not as a classic star or tree. ARCnet systems actually bend this rule a bit. The topology of ARCnet resembles a string of stars or a branching star or a star burst. It might even be considered as a coaxial star. ARCnet does use coaxial cable as a physical medium and will connect hub sites with coax, so it has characteristics of a bus network. Actual user ports, however, are at drop cables radiating out from the actual hub sites, so ARCnet also has characteristics of a star network.

Broadband coaxial cable can be configured as a bus or tree, but not as a star or ring, and optical fiber generally is set up as a star or ring. Star networks require a physical link between each station on the network, and coaxial cable would be horribly clumsy because of its bulk. Twisted pair and fiber optic cable, on the other hand, are well suited to such a topology because of their smaller diameters. Fiber, however, cannot easily be configured as a bus or a tree because of the problem of coupling and splitting signals. Point-to-point is easiest and cheapest with fiber media. That does not mean that cost-effective optical couplers and splitters will not be developed. They just are not economically attractive today. Baseband coaxial networks cannot be configured as trees because they transmit digitally and bidirectionally, and it is very difficult to pass digital signals through splitters and couplers. Technically, broadband transmission techniques could be used for a ring architecture, but such would be expensive and cumbersome.

Twisted pair wire and coaxial cable have been the most commonly used media for LANs, although fiber optic cabling, at some future time, will become more common. Baseband media include twisted pair wiring and 50-Ω coaxial cable. Broadband networks use 75-Ω coaxial cable as a transmission medium. The construction of baseband and broadband cabling is the same construction, but their electrical characteristics are different.

Cost, number of nodes to be connected, distance to be covered, and type of information conveyed on the network will influence the choice of media. Sometimes, especially in factories, resistance to electrical noise and interference generated by mechanical devices and power sources may be an important factor. Each type of medium has advantages and limitations.

Twisted pair wire, consisting of two insulated wires typically made of copper or copper-coated steel and twisted around each other in a spiral pattern, is the same wire used on telephone networks. It is cheap and easy to handle, requiring little technical skill to install and connect devices. But twisted pair offers a limited data rate (64 kb/s to a few megabits) and is susceptible to noise and interference from machinery, unless it is shielded. Also, because its bandwidth is relatively limited, twisted pair is not suited to networks connecting hundreds or thousands of users. Twisted pair is typically used for low-speed applications connecting relatively few users over a star network. However, new products now on the market will run Ethernet over unshielded twisted pair wiring at 10 Mb/s.

Coaxial cable has been used as a LAN medium where communication at higher speeds and over longer distances is required. (See Fig. 1.5.) Coaxial cable has two conductors that share a common center axis. The center conductor carries the signals, and the outer conductor acts as a shield. The center conductor is usually solid copper or copper-clad aluminum, and the outer conductor is usually aluminum. Between the two conductors is a dielectric (insulating material), typically foamed polyethylene. Trilogy Communications, however, makes a trunk cable with an air dielectric. Sometimes polyethylene jackets are added for greater resistance to abrasion and moisture. Flooding compounds are sometimes used between the outer conductor and the jacket when cables are to be run under water or buried. The difference between baseband and broadband coaxial

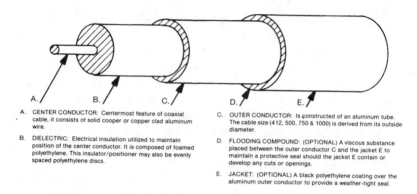

A. **CENTER CONDUCTOR:** Centermost feature of coaxial cable, it consists of solid cooper or copper clad aluminum wire.

B. **DIELECTRIC:** Electrical insulation utilized to maintain position of the center conductor. It is composed of foamed polyethylene. This insulator/positioner may also be evenly spaced polyethylene discs.

C. **OUTER CONDUCTOR:** Is constructed of an aluminum tube. The cable size (412, 500, 750 & 1000) is derived from its outside diameter.

D. **FLOODING COMPOUND:** (OPTIONAL) A viscous substance placed between the outer conductor C and the jacket E to maintain a protective seal should the jacket E contain or develop any cuts or openings.

E. **JACKET:** (OPTIONAL) A black polyethylene coating over the aluminum outer conductor to provide a weather-tight seal.

Figure 1.5 Coaxial cable.

cable is the electrical impedance each has. Baseband uses a 50-Ω cable, and broadband uses 75-Ω cable.

Fiber optic cable has not yet become a major LAN medium, although it has gained wide acceptance as a long-distance point-to-point medium. Recently the American National Standards Institute (ANSI) has proposed a new standard for 100-Mb/s backbone ring networks, known as the *fiber distributed data interface* (FDDI). Operating at 1300 nm over multimode fiber and using laser light sources, FDDI networks will space repeaters every 2 km to form networks with a maximum distance of 200 km. FDDI will be an important fiber LAN standard in the coming years.

Fiber optic cable has a central core of glass or plastic and a surrounding cladding layer of glass or plastic with a refractive index lower than that of the central core. As a ray of light passes from a medium with a higher refractive index to a medium with a lower refractive index, the ray is bent back toward the medium with the higher index of refraction. There are three basic types of fibers: single mode, multimode stepped index, and multimode graded index. Multimode fibers allow light to take a variety of paths as it bounces down the fiber. This results in propagation delay: different rays will bounce at different angles, travel different distances, and thus arrive at the receiver at slightly different times. *Modal dispersion* is the term used to describe the delay. A single-mode fiber, on the other hand, has a core that is so small that only a single path can be taken.

1.2 BANDWIDTH

Bandwidth refers to the range of frequencies that can be carried over a network, and is expressed as the difference between the highest frequency and the lowest frequency. Bandwidth is measured in cycles per second or hertz (Hz). Bandwidth also refers to the data rate in bits per second (b/s) on a digital network: the higher the bandwidth, the greater the information-carrying capacity of the medium. A rule of thumb for figuring bandwidth consumption at various data rates is to allocate 1 Hz for 1 b/s at 5 Mb/s and above and about 2 Hz for each bit per second desired at lower rates. A transmission rate of 5 Mb/s, for example, can easily be handled by 6 MHz of bandwidth. Typically, broadband channels are divided into many slower-speed data channels, however.

1.2.1 Baseband

Consider the term *broadband*, especially as compared to *baseband*. Baseband networks, such as Ethernet or the public telephone system, carry signals that occupy the entire bandwidth of the medium. In other words, only a single channel is available at any time, and the signal is not modulated (mixed) with a carrier. A broadband network, in contrast, carries many channels and many signals simultaneously. Baseband systems impress the actual signal directly onto the carrying medium, commonly as high and low voltage levels. Broadband systems modulate the actual signals with a *radio frequency* (RF) carrier, much as a boxcar might carry a load of freight. The term *wideband* is sometimes used to describe a broadband medium. Fiber optic systems can use either a broadband or a baseband signaling technique. The typical telephone network use is digital and baseband. The emerging CATV use of fiber is analog and broadband.

Baseband signaling is digital, occupies the entire bandwidth of the cable, and can run up to 10 Mb/s. Broadband systems can accept either analog or digital signaling, although analog is usually chosen.

Connecting devices to a broadband LAN requires the use of a *modem* (a contraction of the term *modulator-demodulator*). A modem receives a modulated RF carrier signal and strips away the carrier to produce the actual digital or analog signal. A modem also has the ability to modulate outgoing signals with an RF carrier for transmission. The requirement for modulation and demodulation ability is one reason why a broadband modem costs more than a baseband transceiver. The transceiver simply puts a voltage stream directly onto the network without modulating it.

Modulation (See Fig. 1.6) simply means the mixing of information, either digital bits or analog information like TV signals, with an RF carrier. Recall that an RF carrier has three characteristics: frequency of oscillation, amplitude of oscillation, and phase of oscillation. *Frequency* refers to how often a carrier wave oscillates, or vibrates, in a given time (the faster the oscillation, the higher the frequency). *Amplitude* refers to the size of a

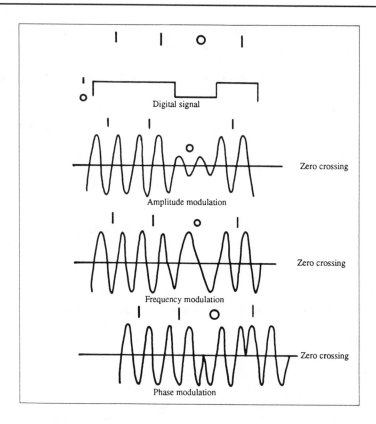

Figure 1.6 Modulation formats.

carrier measured from positive peak to negative peak (the taller the waves, the higher the amplitude). *Phase* refers to timing when a wave crosses the zero point between its positive and negative oscillations. The time difference between two identical waves going through their positive peaks is called *phase*.

It is the use of the RF carrier that gives broadband its greater system reach. Recall that the RF technology used for broadband LANs is similar to the RF technology used to broadcast TV signals over the air and to send satellite signals through space. In each case, a desired signal is mixed with a higher-power RF carrier before transmission.

Baseband systems are digital and transmit bidirectionally. Broadband systems are analog and transmit only in a single direction on any channel or frequency. A signal inserted into a baseband network will propagate to both ends of the bus. A signal inserted on a broadband network always travels back toward the headend, while all received signals come from the headend.

Baseband systems use digital, or discrete, signaling techniques. Broadband systems use analog, or continuous, signaling. Digital signaling uses discrete methods to convey information: high and low voltage, on and off, ones and zeros. All information is conveyed as a series of binary states. Analog signaling uses continuously varying states of change, from a maximum value to a minimum value, to convey information—waves and oscillations, for example—rather than binary on-off changes.

1.3 ACCESS PROTOCOLS

Because many stations can transmit at any point in time on many LANs (bus and tree LANs in particular), some method has to be used to control access to the network. The terms *deterministic system* and *contention system* are often used to describe access methods. Token passing and polling are said to be deterministic, whereas CSMA/CD, Aloha, or slotted Aloha are said to be random access or contention methods. Technically, though, even token and polling systems are somewhat probabilistic in terms of access time to the network for any given message from any given station. Perhaps it is more accurate to say that there are three access methods. Truly deterministic systems might be those that allocate access by *time-division multiplexing* (TDM), in which each user has a given time slot available for transmission. Controlled access would include token passing and polling methods. Token passing might be seen as a form of distributed polling, in fact.

Roll call polling, where one station has the role of central controller, is a form of controlled access. In a roll call polling network all stations are interrogated sequentially by a central controller. A typical application is telemetry, where a single controller polls temperature sensors or security stations in turn, interrogating each station for data. This type of polling works well for gathering data from remote terminals on a batch basis.

Hub polling involves the transfer of access control from one station to the next in sequential order. A central controller might poll the furthest station first. This station would transmit its message and append the address of its neighbor to the inbound message. This station would, in turn, add any message of its own and append the address of the next station in the inbound path. The process would be repeated until all stations have reached the controller. Then the process would begin again. This sounds a lot like token passing. Token passing really is a sort of hub polling, except that messages from neighboring stations are not appended. Instead, each station transmits its own complete message before surrendering the access token to the next station in line.

Random access is another method for controlling terminal access to a network. A contention system allows terminals to compete with each other for access to the network, and it requires no central controller. Examples of contention networks are the CSMA/CD, Aloha, and slotted Aloha systems. Contention systems work best when traffic on the network is light to moderate and messages are short and bursty, or where there are only a few host computers communicating with each other. Where tight control of access delay is critical, such as in the manufacturing environment, controlled access is preferred. Contention networks are robust, since there is no single point of failure other than a severing of the cable or a terminal malfunction causing the transmission of a continuous stream of data without end. The throughput rates for contention systems are high compared with circuit switching systems, and it is relatively simple to add or rearrange stations.

On the other hand, contention access begins to suffer throughput limitations as network load rises, because more collisions occur. In addition, the relationship between overhead bits and information bits in each transmitted packet makes a difference. Asynchronous transmission formats, which do not use common clocking for transmitters and receivers, require start and stop bits, for example. Network size also contributes to throughput limitations. Longer cable runs mean longer transit times for information, and therefore a bigger collision window.

The *window* is the period of time during which a transmitting station cannot tell whether another station at the opposite end of the network has begun transmitting. Although electricity travels through coaxial cable at about three quarters of the speed of light, some propagation time is still required. The collision window basically consists of the amount of time it takes a signal to travel to the furthest stations on the network.

For these and other reasons, regarding medium access time, contention systems are less predictable than controlled access systems, although, strictly speaking, all access methods except TDM are statements of probabilities. Access time on a contention network can be stated only as a probability under certain conditions of loading, with heavy loads requiring more time than light loads do. It is not possible to say exactly how long a terminal will take to send a message.

One of the oldest and most widely used contention systems on bus systems is CSMA/CD. In the CSMA/CD system a station with a message to send listens to the other stations to determine if any are transmitting. If another station is transmitting, the listening station waits. If no station is transmitting, the message may be sent immediately. This protocol can be called a "listen before transmitting" system. However, it is possible that two stations may hear nothing and thus begin transmitting at the same time. When that happens, the signals collide. With CSMA/CD, transmitting stations listen for collisions; if the stations detect collisions, they stop transmitting and wait a random (pseudorandom in some cases) time before transmitting again.

The Ethernet and IEEE 802.3 standards use a retransmission algorithm, called *binary exponential backoff* (See Fig. 1.7), to increase the random number chosen for retransmission, based on not the number of stations on the network but on the amount of traffic. Stations on lightly loaded networks wait less time before retransmitting than do stations on heavily loaded networks.

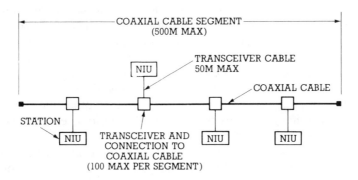

Figure 1.7 Single Ethernet cable segment configuration. (Courtesy of Ungermann-Bass, Inc.)

Under some conditions, such as factory assembly line or food processing operations, it is vital that network access time be more strictly defined, because process control operations must take place sequentially and in real time. Also, when traffic is very heavy and messages are very long, the only way to ensure higher throughput is to regulate access more closely. Polling, for example, is a form of regulated access, as is circuit switching and token passing.

The Aloha system is a simple system in which all users transmit at will. When a collision is detected, the stations involved attempt to retransmit the entire message on a staggered basis in time, as dictated by a collision-resolution algorithm. Aloha systems quickly become unstable as the number of network users and transmission frequency increases. Maximum throughput is about 18% of line capacity.

Slotted Aloha improves throughput about 100% by synchronizing all the terminals in time and allowing transmissions only at the beginning of time slots that it defines. Transmissions are allowed at N, $2N$, $3N$, $4N$, and so forth, so that collisions can occur only when two or more stations decide to transmit at the beginning of one of the time slots.

Token passing is a more deterministic method for regulating access to the network, and has been chosen as the access method for MAP networks, which are token-passing bus LANs. A control packet called the *token* regulates access to the network: no station may transmit unless it possesses the token. When a station gets the token, it is authorized to transmit one or more messages for a specified time. When transmission is finished, or when the maximum alloted time is reached, the token must be passed to the next station. Only the transmitting node can remove the message from the network, because, when a receiving station has gotten the message addressed to it, an acknowledgement message is added to the packet as it recirculates. When the transmitting station gets the token again and sees the acknowledgement message, the station knows the message has gotten through and it can remove the message from the token, thereby freeing the token for use by the next station on the ring.

Token networks use minimum time for network control because all stations are programmed not to interfere with each other: no token, no transmit. On contention networks, overhead (collisions, error messages, retransmit delays) increases as the volume of traffic increases. A token-passing system, by way of contrast, consists of nothing but overhead when the token is circulating and nobody is talking. Yet it becomes more efficient as an information carrier as load increases: more of the volume consists of actual messages; less consists of token overhead. Token networks also can be bigger because each node is a repeater and because there is no collision window to worry about.

On the other hand, token-passing systems are vulnerable whenever a token is lost or damaged, typically when a node fails while it has the token. When this happens the ring has to be reinitialized. Since any station might fail, all other stations need the ability to reinitialize all other stations. A token-passing bus behaves just like a token ring: each station knows the identity of the stations preceding it and following it, and the token is always passed in turn as though the network were an actual ring.

When traffic is light and few users are on a network, random access networks will outperform controlled access networks. Under such conditions, the number of collisions is likely to be so small that the actual throughput, defined as the actual transit time of the messages through the network from port to port, is almost minimal. Polling and token-passing access schemes, by way of contrast, have overhead associated with them even when no station is transmitting. The token still has to be passed from node to node, or the central controller has to interrogate each node in turn.

Under light loads contention system traffic consists mostly of information and contains little overhead, whereas controlled access system traffic under light load is mostly overhead. Under heavy loads the reverse is true. A contention system experiences more and more collisions, and therefore more of the actual traffic on the network is overhead. A controlled access system, on the other hand, becomes more efficient under heavy loads: overhead remains stable while the actual information carried steadily increases as a proportion of total traffic.

1.4 STANDARDS

Although most LANs originally used proprietary access and transmission schemes, there is increasing international standardization of communication and hardware standards, spurred by the activities of diverse groups such as the International Standards Organization (ISO), a voluntary group consisting of national standards committees from member countries. The ISO works to set standards for encryption, data communications, and public data networks. The ISO has popularized the *open systems interconnection* (OSI) model, a seven-layer software protocol designed to ease interconnection and interoperability of equipment made by various manufacturers.

Another important standards body is ANSI, a member of the ISO and the national standards group for the United States. ANSI set the standards for Cobol and FORTRAN programming languages.

At the interface level, the Electronic Industries Association (EIA), a national trade organization, focuses its attention on electrical standards such as RS-232 and RS-449.

The National Bureau of Standards (NBS) makes recommendations on federal data processing and communications standards and has been active in testing the MAP, an international standard compliant with the OSI model and adapted for factory-automation systems.

The Federal Telecommunications Standards Committee (FTSC) is an interagency group with the charge of setting and maintaining standards for government-purchased communications equipment. The focus is on interoperability, especially at the lower levels of the OSI protocol stack.

The Defense Communications Agency (DCA) is another federal body concerned with standards for communications equipment, but it focuses on military applications. It publishes its rules as military standards (MIL-STD).

User groups recently have become more important in the standards arena. The MAP, an international standard for communication and automation systems in industrial settings, originally was pioneered by General Motors and now is spearheaded by the Society of Manufacturing Engineers

(SME). MAP is based on the OSI model. A related effort started by Boeing is known as the *technical and office protocols* (TOP). A companion standard to MAP, TOP is designed as a set of standards for front office and engineering computing environments that can interface with MAP systems in the factory. Also based on the OSI model, TOP development now is led by the SME.

In 1986 a nonprofit organization called the Corporation for Open Systems (COS) was established by 60 major vendors of data processing and data communication equipment. COS works to speed adoption of equipment and software conforming to the OSI model and seeks interoperability of equipment that meets OSI standards. COS is currently concentrating on uniform test standards and certification procedures for equipment and software that is designed to be OSI-compliant.

Among the more important influences on LAN standards, aside from the OSI standards, are those set by the computer society of the Institute of Electrical and Electronics Engineers (IEEE) and ANSI. These organizations have codified a number of important LAN standards collectively known as 802 standards. Standard 802.1 describes how the 802 family of standards complies with the OSI model. Standard 802.2 deals with medium access standards for all 802 family networks. The 802.3 standard deals with bus networks using the CSMA/CD access method. Ethernet is almost identical to the 802.3 standard, and the developing TOP, which are designed as a front office companion to MAP, also use 802.3 standards. The 802.4 standards deal with token-passing bus networks, which MAP is based on. The 802.5 standard sets protocols for token-passing ring networks such as the IBM token ring network. The 802.6 committee is looking at standards for MANs (using CATV and possibly fiber optic technology). The 802.7 committee is developing standards for broadband LANs. Draft specifications now circulating indicate an analog signaling format with a 10-Mb/s token ring structure similar to a token ring.

1.4.1 The OSI Model

The OSI model and IEEE 802 committee standards are increasingly essential to understanding where LAN technology is going. Both are concerned with standardizing the process by which computing devices made by different vendors can communicate. Commonly referred to as an *open systems* model, because it allows connection of any two or more systems conforming to the reference model, the OSI is a layered set of standards in which each layer plays a distinct part in setting up and maintaining a communications link. (See Fig. 1.8.) The idea is to compartmentalize the functions of the layers in such a way that the higher layers depend on the

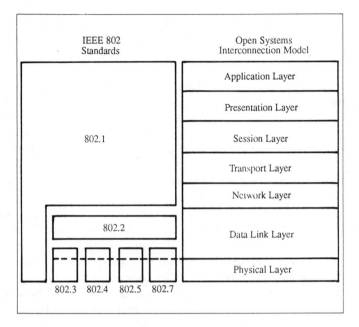

Figure 1.8 OSI model.

transparent functioning of the lower layers. Ideally, one ought to be able to revise the software for any layer without affecting the operation of the remaining layers.

The first layer, the *physical layer*, sets electrical parameters for the cable or wire and actual interface that have been selected as the transmission medium. Such details as signal voltage durations and swings, assignments of functions to pins used in connectors, and all mechanical and electrical requirements to establish a device-level communications link are covered by this set of protocols. The common RS-232 and RS-449 standards are examples of physical layer specifications.

Link layer is the second layer of the OSI stack. It is concerned with the reliable maintenance of a data communication link, and takes care of the detection and correction of data transmission errors. The data link layer activates, maintains, and deactivates communication links. It creates data frames, processes acknowledgement messages from the receiver, and sets flags and headers so that the receiving terminal can recognize the start and end of data frames. When an error has been detected, the data link layer has the job of sending a retransmission request to the transmitting terminal. The data link layer also handles message addressing. *Cyclic redundancy checking* (CRC), a common method of comparing transmitted with received data streams to detect errors, is handled at the data link layer. The protocols known as *high-level data link control* (HDLC) and IBM's *synchronous data link control* (SDLC) are examples of data link protocols.

The third layer is the *network layer*, which is concerned with the transparent transmission of data packets on a network. The network layer gets messages from the higher layers, breaks them into packets, delivers them to their destinations, and reassembles them in original form. The packet-switching protocol X.25 is an example of software at the network layer.

The fourth layer is called the *transport layer*. This layer establishes and terminates connections between communicating devices. The transport layer ensures that data is delivered without errors and in the proper sequence, without bit losses or bit duplications. Flow control and error handling also occur at this layer. Flow control can be thought of as a gatekeeper on the on-ramp of a freeway, regulating vehicles as they merge with traffic already on the freeway. Message headers and control messages are embedded by the transport layer on packets being sent between terminals, thus ensuring integrity of the communication link between the two devices. The transport layer also has the task of selecting the most appropriate available transmission network for sending a message: public telephone network, satellite network, packet-switching network, or LAN, for example.

The fifth layer is the *session layer*, which determines whether devices can interrupt each other; it establishes rules for starting and ending a communication and for reestablishing a connection that has been interrupted. This layer also checks for user authenticity, provides a billing record, and decides whether the communication ought to be full- or half-duplex.

The *presentation layer*, the sixth layer, interprets the data streams flowing between terminals and adjusts them, if required, for syntax (data formats and signal levels). Code conversion, text compression, and standardized layouts for printers and terminals are governed by the presentation layer. This layer is necessary because different machines have different character sets, data formats, and structures. The presentation layer reformats received data so that the application layer can understand it. Encryption services would be provided at this layer.

The *application layer*, the seventh layer, is the least standardized layer. Basically, the application layer provides access to the OSI environment for an actual applications package. The layer decides what task must be performed so that the user can run a particular program, for example, word processing or facsimile transmission.

1.4.2   The 802 Standards

The IEEE's 802 standards are an important set of LAN standards and are compliant with, but not identical to, the OSI model. The IEEE standards only deal with the two lowest levels of the OSI model: the physical and logical link control layers. The IEEE began work on the 802 family of LAN standards in 1980, and work continues today on the 802.3, 802.6, and 802.7 standards. The 802.2 logical link control standard is media-independent. Three different physical layer and medium access standards were set, however. The 802.3 standard specifies the use of CSMA/CD access protocols on a bus network, the 802.4 standard specifies the use of token access on a bus network, and the 802.5 standard specifies the use of token access on a ring network. The 802.6 and 802.7 standards are not officially released yet, although the 802.7 broadband network standard is circulating as a draft international standard. The actual physical layer specification is not precisely specified yet. A group also is working on fiber optic technical standards under the umbrella of the 802.8 subcommittee. Another subcommittee, the 802.9 group, is working on integrated data and voice networks.

The 802.3 standard contention bus uses the CSMA/CD form of access protocol. This protocol is a refinement of Ethernet, which was in turn a refinement of the Aloha system originally developed at the University of Hawaii. Aloha was a contention-based RF network in which all stations transmitted toward a master station on one frequency; the master station broadcast messages to secondary stations on another frequency. Because messages often collided with each other, stations were instructed to wait a random time after collisions occurred before they retransmitted. As a result, actual throughput was only about 18.4%. A refinement called slotted Aloha was then developed, which added synchronization of all secondary stations to a master clock. Throughput was thus improved to about 36.8 percent.

The 802.3 standard uses a variation of the Aloha concepts, but also requires that all stations listen for any other transmissions in progress and hold transmissions until the channel is clear. Using 802.3, stations also continue to monitor the channel for evidence that a collision has occurred. If a collision is detected, each transmitting station waits a random time before attempting to send its message again. Ethernet (Fig. 1.9), the popular baseband LAN technology, uses an 802.3 compliant protocol (although Ethernet and 802.3 are not totally identical), as does the new TOP protocol.

Signaling is at the rate of 10 Mb/s. For baseband implementations of the Ethernet specification, a single *medium access unit* (MAU) can send

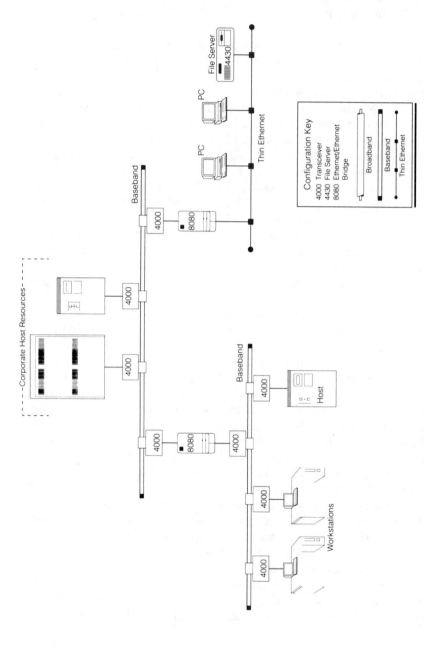

Figure 1.9 Broadband Ethernet implementation. (Courtesy of Sytek.)

a signal a distance of up to 500 m (no individual cable path can exceed 500 m in length). The longest path between any two transceivers (MAUs) is 1500 m. Repeater units are used to extend the range of an Ethernet network, and no more than two repeater units may be in the path between any two MAUs. The 802.3 specification allows as many as four repeater units between any two MAUs. In addition, a point-to-point link between repeaters cannot be longer than 1000 m. No more than 1024 stations may be on the network, and no more than 100 can be attached to any single segment of cable. (The MAU assumes a data collision has occurred when the signal level on the cable equals or exceeds that produced by two transmitters.)

The broadband specification for MAUs has not been formally released yet, but details should conform closely to the following. The functions of the MAU are to transmit serial data in a band-limited modulated RF carrier format, receive a modulated RF data signal and demodulate it to a bit stream, and detect collisions and interrupt itself if it begins transmitting an unusually long data stream. This interruption is known as the *jabber function*, a method for detecting a faulty transmitter that is locked on transmit and is sending data without end.

The MAU receive level is set at nominal 6 dBmV, with a low of -4 dBmV and a maximum of 16 dBmV. The receiver must be able to operate in a cable environment loaded with signals every 6 MHz. Transmitted signals are *binary phase-shift keyed* (BPSK). Data bandwidth is 14 MHz with an adjacent collision enforcement band 4 MHz wide (a total of 18 MHz). On single-cable systems the 192.25-MHz translation offset is recommended, although 156.25-MHz translation is also permissible. On dual-cable systems, transmit and receive frequencies are identical, running from 36 to 276 MHz.

There are several versions of the 802.3 standard, depending on the medium used to transport the signals. The original 50-Ω coaxial cable specification is called *10BASE5* and calls for a 10-Mb/s data rate using digital signaling and Manchester encoding. A maximum of 100 stations is allowed, and spacing of all stations is a multiple of 2.5 m. Maximum network length is defined as 500 m.

The *10BASE2* specification (Fig. 1.10) also uses 50-Ω coaxial cable and the 10-Mb/s signaling rate. Called *Cheapernet*, the 10BASE2 is a less costly implementation for several reasons. The cable used is not as well shielded as the 10BASE5 version. It is thinner and more flexible, easier to bend around corners and, thus, is easier to install. The more flexible cable is less costly as well. Cheapernet cable connects directly to a station, whereas the 10BASE5 version requires a transceiver to connect a station to the network. That means the physical layer components are built right

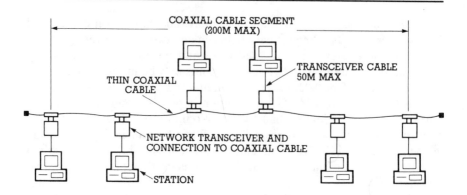

Figure 1.10 10BASE2 network. (Courtesy of Ungermann-Bass, Inc.)

into the station itself, eliminating the external transceiver cabling and interface logic.

Because it uses less shielding, the Cheapernet cable introduces more noise into the system and limits the number of nodes and maximum network distance traversed. The thinner cable also causes more signal attenuation, again reducing total system reach. Both 10BASE5 and 10BASE2 segments can be linked on the same network by a special repeater that conforms to 10BASE5 on one side and 10BASE2 on the other.

The *10BROAD36* specification is a broadband version of Ethernet using standard 75-Ω CATV coaxial cable and running in either a single-cable or a dual-cable version. (See Fig. 1.11.) The maximum segment length is 1800 m, and total system reach is about 3600 m for any single network. Multiple networks can be joined by bridges, and the data rate is 10 Mb/s. The original specification called for a 14-MHz bandwidth and a 4-MHz collision-enforcement channel, for a total bandwidth of 18 MHz. But more bandwidth-efficient 12-MHz implementations are now available from Chipcom Corp. and other companies.

The 1BASE5 version of the standard is an even lower-cost variant than Cheapernet, and uses unshielded twisted pair wire as the network medium. Designed primarily for smaller PC networks, it runs at 1 Mb/s rather than the original 10 Mb/s. Known as *StarLAN*, this version also uses a star topology rather than a bus topology. The single hub serves as a repeater for all stations on the network and performs signal regeneration, signal timing, and collision detection. The maximum distance between any station and the hub is set at 250 m. The maximum network span is 500 m. However, multiple hub levels can be linked together to form a larger network up to 2500 m in length (See Fig. 1.12). In such a multiple-hub network there is one header hub and one or more intermediate hubs. Each

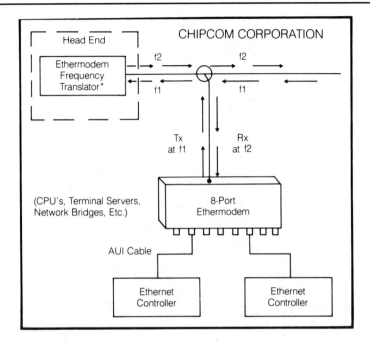

Figure 1.11 10BROAD36 version of Ethernet. (Courtesy of Chipcom Corporation.)

hub can have stations and other hubs attached to it. This type of network is well suited to multiple floors of a single building.

Ethernet is similar, but not identical, to 802.3 networks. Ethernet version 2.0 and 802.3 have a "heartbeat" function that confirms that a given station's collision signaling system is operational. The older Ethernet version 1.0 does not have this function.

Both 802.3 networks and version 2.0 Ethernets have a jabber function to disable any station that transmits continuously or for more than the maximum frame size. This function is designed to disable any station that may have a fault that causes it to transmit endlessly.

Frame formats are different. Ethernet does not have a field length identifier; 802.3 networks do. The organization of the 802.2 logical link layer functions differs from the equivalent portions of an Ethernet frame. Ethernet also handles link and *medium access control* (MAC) functions differently than 802.3 networks do.

The 802.3 standard suggests that it is designed for use in commercial and light industrial applications.

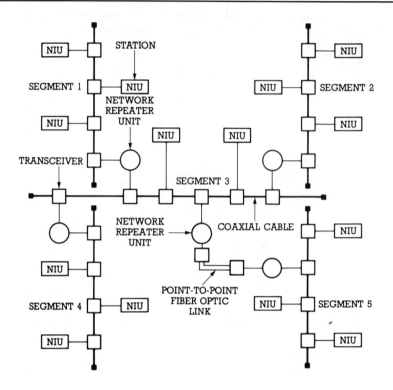

Figure 1.12 Linked Ethernets using repeaters. (Courtesy of Ungermann-Bass, Inc.)

1.4.3 The Token Bus

The 802.4 standard often is referred to as the *token bus standard.* Stations on such a network form a logical ring, although the topology used is that of a tree (bus). All stations are in an ordered sequence, and each station knows the address of the stations immediately before and after it. An 802.4 network is significantly more complicated than an 802.3 network. At least one station (and quite often each station) on the network must have the ability to initialize the ring when it is first started up or after it has crashed. Some means has to be provided for deciding which station goes first and which follow. A strategy for periodically adding new stations to the network is also needed, as well as a way for stations to leave the network. If an error occurs that destroys the circulating token or produces two tokens, some recovery method is required to authenticate one of the duplicate tokens or to create a new one. Also helpful is the ability to rank messages according to priority and to give some classes of messages preference for transmission.

The 802.4 standard (Fig. 1.13) used by MAP is a deterministic protocol, in contrast to the CSMA/CD contention protocol. Based on broadband coaxial cable technology, 802.4 networks control access to the network by requiring that any station wishing to transmit a message be in physical possession of a transmit token. The token passes around to each station on the network in turn. Each station knows the addresses of its predecessor which passed the token and the successor station to which the token is to be passed. Each station also knows its own address. Tokens are passed around the network in numerically descending station address order, regardless of the physical positions of stations on the bus.

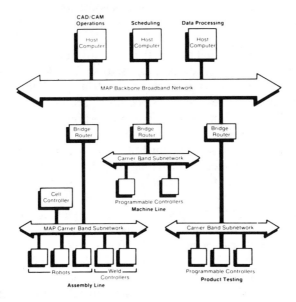

Figure 1.13 802.4 Network.

Three types of modulation formats are specified. One deals with signals running on the broadband trunk system and uses amplitude modulated and phase-shifted signals. This is the "full broadband" portion of the network. The other two modulation and physical layer formats cover the "carrier-band" portions of the network. Unlike the signals carried on the broadband backbone, carrier-band signals are single-channel, not multichannel.

Carrier band offers lower cost connection for work-group or device cell attachment to the broadband network because it does not use the more complex broadband modems. Carrier-band networks do not require frequency translation either. Up to 32 stations are supported on any single carrier-band network at a maximum distance of 700 m. Also, the 802.4 specification recommends two carrier-band formats: one is permanently dedicated to carrier-band technology, and the other can be upgraded to full broadband by a simple switchout of the modems.

Single-channel phase-continuous frequency-shift keying (FSK) is the first of the carrier-band formats. Phase-continuous FSK is a form of modulation where two different frequencies are used to represent the binary 1 and 0 bits and the frequency changes continuously. The trunk cables are standard 75-Ω coaxial cable, but drop cables are 35- to 50-Ω cable and use BNC-type 50-Ω connectors. A signaling rate of 1 Mb/s is recommended. The carrier center frequency is set at 5 MHz, with oscillations running between 3.75 and 6.25 MHz. Output levels for modems are 54–60 dB. This variant of carrier band is not designed to be upgraded to full broadband.

Although not a formal part of the standard, it is good practice to not use repeaters and to keep drops (no less than 2 and no more than 30), extending from a single trunk cable, as short as possible. The reason is that each drop causes reflections, since drops are not matched or terminated, and the size of the reflection is proportional to the length of the drop.

Single-channel phase-coherent FSK is the second carrier-band modulation format and relates the signaling frequencies to the data rate, with transitions between the two frequencies being made at the zero crossings of the carrier waveform. A 75-Ω cable is used for both trunk and drop cables, allowing either a 5-Mb/s or a 10-Mb/s signaling rate. The use of standard CATV components means that a carrier-band network using phase-coherent FSK can be upgraded to full broadband. Output levels are set between 60 and 63 dB, and 75-Ω F-type connectors are used on the drops. At the 5-Mb/s signaling rate, the lower tone is set at 5 MHz, the higher tone at 10 MHz. When the 10 Mb/s signaling rate is desired, the lower tone is set at 10 MHz, the upper tone at 20 MHz.

Unlike the phase-continuous carrier-band application, which uses 50-Ω cable, the phase-coherent version of the standard specifies a branched tree topology instead of a single-cable bus. The 75-Ω version of carrier band uses standard CATV-type power supplies, power combining passives, and nondirectional taps, rather than standard CATV-type directional taps.

This particular form of carrier band is designed for upgrading to full broadband plant by replacing the carrier-band modems with broadband modems and by adding amplifiers or a headend remodulator if necessary. The full broadband specification requires *amplitude modulated phase-shift keying* (AM PSK). Also known as *duobinary signaling*, AM PSK involves an amplitude modulated RF carrier and a phase-shift-keyed carrier. The

802.4 specification uses a multilevel duobinary AM PSK having three amplitude levels instead of two. Signaling rates of 1, 5, and 10 Mb/s are possible. The 1-Mb/s rate uses 1.5 MHz per channel; the 5 Mb/s uses 6 MHz per channel; and the 10 Mb/s rate uses 12 MHz per channel. The 192.25-MHz translation offset is recommended.

The 802.4 standard does not specify where token bus systems are best used. Industrial and military applications seem to predominate, however.

1.4.4 Token Ring

The 802.5 standard often is referred to as the token ring standard. It supports data rates of 1 Mb/s and 4 Mb/s using differential Manchester encoding. The physical medium used is a 150-Ω shielded twisted pair wire. The IBM token ring network, running at 4 Mb/s on 150-Ω twisted pair media and 16 Mb/s on fiber optic cable, is an 802.5 network. IBM also supports a broadband cable version running at 4, 20, and 40 Mb/s. The IBM token ring network runs a recommended 72 nodes when unshielded twisted pair wire is used and 260 nodes when shielded twisted pair wire is used.

Like 802.3 LANs, the 802.5 standard suggests that token ring networks are best suited to commercial and light industrial applications. Like the token bus system, access is gained by means of a bit pattern called a *token* that circulates around the ring when all stations are idle. Any station wishing to transmit must wait for possession of the token. When it has the token, the station can append a message to the token before retransmitting it to the next station on the ring. All stations on the ring listen for their own address header when they get possession of the token. When the intended recipient station has read the message, it inserts an acknowledgement message. When the transmitting station again gets the token, it looks for the acknowledgement message. Receiving the message, the transmitting station purges the address header and inserts a clean token.

Under light loading the amount of overhead is rather high compared to the amount of data being transmitted, since each station must wait for the token before transmitting. Under heavy load, however, efficiency increases. An eight-level priority system is also part of the access algorithm. Basically, a station having a higher priority than that used by the current frame can reserve the next token at a higher level as the token passes by. When the current station is finished transmitting, it issues the token at the requested higher priority. Stations with messages at lower priorities are prevented from seizing the token. The station responsible for upgrading the priority level is required to downgrade the priority level to its original setting, once the station has established that all messages with higher priority have been transmitted by all stations on the ring.

The 802.6 standard covers MANs running on fiber optic cable. Coaxial cable standards originally had been considered for this standard, but there was no interest on the part of CATV operators, who run such networks.

The 802.7 specification is expected to address both single-cable and dual-cable broadband networks and to explain how the standard relates to the 802.3 and 802.4 standards as well.

1.4.5 FDDI

The FDDI, a 100-Mb/s fiber optic ring network based on the 802.5 standard, is a new proposed standard for backbone, backend, and high-speed office networks. Backend networks are used to connect main-frame computers and mass storage devices in computer room environments where reliable bulk data transfer among a limited number of devices in a small area is needed.

High-speed office networks will be increasingly in demand because of the growth of desktop imaging devices, such as facsimile machines, document image processors, and graphics programs (*computer-aided design* (CAD), *computer-aided engineering* (CAE), and *computer-aided manufacturing* (CAM)). As optical disk storage becomes more prevalent, high-speed data transfer requirements will likewise rise.

Backbone networks are used for premises-wide networks on campuses, military bases, industrial and research parks, and large manufacturing and industrial facilities. The function is to provide a high-speed, high-bandwidth network that operates on a facility-wide basis to interconnect dispersed subnetworks. The approach is to confine localized traffic to each separate LAN while using the backbone for traffic that moves from one subnetwork to another.

Although based on the 802.5 standard, the FDDI is quite different from the token ring network. FDDI uses fiber optic media; token ring uses shielded twisted pair. FDDI runs at 100 Mb/s; token ring runs at either 1 Mb/s or 4 Mb/s. FDDI uses a *nonreturn to zero* (NRZ) encoding scheme; token ring networks use *differential Manchester* encoding. FDDI uses distributed clocking; token ring employs centralized clocking. The frame structures, token insertion windows, token rotation times, and frame sizes also are different.

The basic access method is similar, however. When all stations are idle, a token frame circulates to all stations on the ring. When a station wishes to transmit, it waits for the token, appends a message, and transmits. When the token and appended message have made a complete circuit of the ring, the transmitting station removes the message and frees the token for use by another station. A station holding the transmit token can send messages until all the data is gone or until a token-holding timing limit is reached.

The FDDI protocol provides for a specialized and extended session format between any two stations on the network. A station wishing to have an extended session with another station can issue a restricted token. When the destination station gets the regular nonrestricted token, the first frame of data, and the restricted token, that station alone can transmit further asynchronous frames on the network. The restricted token is passed back and forth between the two stations having the extended session until the session is ended. All stations on an FDDI network share responsibility for monitoring the network for faults requiring initialization of the ring.

Signals on an FDDI network are intensity modulated by *light-emitting diodes* (LEDs) operating at the 1300-nm wavelength over multimode fiber. Maximum distance between any two repeaters is set at 2 km, with a maximum of 100 nodes and a total network span of 200 km.

The FDDI standard is not being developed by an 802 committee but by the Accredited Standards Committee for Information Processing System (ASC X3), a quasi-independent group sponsored by the Computer and Business Equipment Manufacturers Association (CBEMA), a trade group representing information processing, communications, and business products vendors, under the umbrella of ANSI. The FDDI protocol is a proposed ANSI standard.

1.4.6 TCP/IP

Without question, there will be a migration to OSI standards by major LAN and WAN system vendors. At present, however, there also is a growing use of the Department of Defense (DoD) protocol suite known as the *transmission control protocol/internet protocol* (TCP/IP). The TCP/IP suite originally was developed to support DoD's ARPAnet (Advanced Research Projects Agency) communication network (the world's first packet-switching network), and support for TCP/IP protocols now is required for all military communication procurements. TCP/IP has become an important protocol suite for the university community. The TCP was designed for connecting dissimilar computers and computing devices over packet-switched networks or sets of packet-switching networks.

The TCP/IP protocols are designed to serve two major classes of networks: LANs and WANs. At the local level, host computers are networked together and communicate with other networks through gateways or routers.

TCP itself is designed to support the transparent and reliable transfer of data between networks and devices in full-duplex mode. As with the OSI model, TCP fits in the middle of the protocol stack: below the higher-level application and presentation layers, but above the physical, data link, and network layers.

Known as MIL-STD-1778, TCP is a transport protocol responsible for ensuring a reliable transmission of data between two computers or computing devices. Typically, error correction is handled at this level. Multiplexing services (support of multiple users), connection management (make the connection at the appropriate level of security and order of precedence; maintain the viability of the link; close the link and end), and actual data transport (maintain the bidirectional flow of data between the devices; maintain the same sequence of data as originally transmitted; check for errors) are handled at the transport level.

The IP, MIL-STD-1777, was developed to handle the network layer functions generally corresponding to the first three OSI layers (physical, data link, network). The function of the IP is to pass data between hosts on an *internetwork*, an interconnected set of networks. The IP does not guarantee that all data will be delivered, nor can it guarantee that the delivered data will be in the correct sequence. That function is reserved for the TCP, but the IP is flexible in dealing with differing networks and is relatively quick because it routes data by the most efficient path. When a station wishes to transmit a message to a terminal on another network, the IP has the job of recognizing that the message is destined for the other network and adding an appropriate address header. It then sends the message to the appropriate gateway. At the gateway a routing decision is made. If the message is too large, it is broken up into smaller packets and each packet is queued for transmission and sent. Because differing networks transmit and receive at different rates, the IP contains flow control mechanisms that can adjust the rates at which gateways transmit and receive data.

As OSI-compliant data transmission systems become more popular, TCP/IP is correspondingly projected to shrink in popularity. At the moment, however, full OSI implementations are not widespread and TCP/IP is enjoying a major burst of new support. It should become an increasingly important and popular standard for broadband backbone networks.

1.5 GATEWAYS AND BRIDGES

Broadband is an appropriate technology for linking multiple LANs at a single enterprise. But to link diverse LANs requires the use of one or more types of relays (a *relay* is an intermediary device that connects networks). Four major categories of relays operate at different levels of the OSI protocol model. *Repeaters* (Fig 1.14) connect two similar LAN segments at the physical level and simply extend the LAN's geographic area of coverage. The repeater amplifies (in broadband terminology a repeater is known as an amplifier) reshapes, and retimes signals (if required) before sending them to the next network segment.

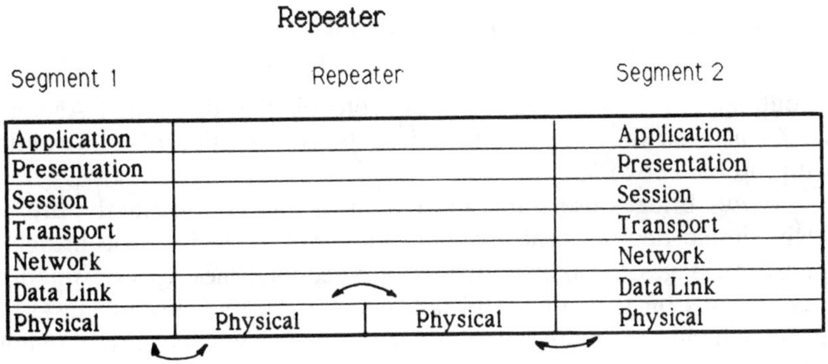

Repeater

Segment 1	Repeater		Segment 2
Application			Application
Presentation			Presentation
Session			Session
Transport			Transport
Network			Network
Data Link			Data Link
Physical	Physical	Physical	Physical

Figure 1.14 Repeaters operate at the physical layer.

A *bridge* (Fig. 1.15) is a relay that can join two networks or network segments at the data link layer (layer 2). When a bridge is used, there is no need for additional data link headers appended to messages. Two addresses, and only two are appended to the message: the source address and the destination address. Bridges that join IEEE 802–type LANs directly are called *local* bridges. When 802-type LANs are connected at long distance, *remote* bridges are used. The remote bridge transfers data from a LAN to a long-haul network of some kind.

Unlike most repeaters, a bridge can perform media protocol conversion. It contains the intelligence to route messages intended for stations on another network segment and to confine messages intended for stations on the same network segment. A bridge can also be used to connect two similar LANs when the use of a repeater would exceed the maximum propagation delay time allowed by the network. Often a bridge is referred to as *MAC-level*. MAC-level bridges are important because they operate

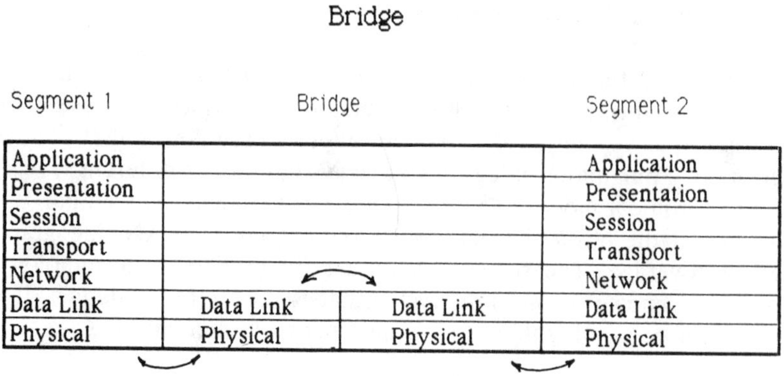

Bridge

| | Segment 1 | Bridge | | Segment 2 |

Segment 1	Bridge		Segment 2
Application			Application
Presentation			Presentation
Session			Session
Transport			Transport
Network			Network
Data Link	Data Link	Data Link	Data Link
Physical	Physical	Physical	Physical

Figure 1.15 Bridges operate at the data link layer.

without reference to the higher-level protocols that different LANs may use. As a result they are well suited to the construction of multivendor, multiprotocol networks.

Simple bridges use static address tables and, consequently, are relatively simple devices. The table of addresses is used by the bridge to forward messages to other networks or to confine messages destined for other stations on the same network segment. Reconfiguration tasks, on the other hand, are more complex for simple bridges, because moving a station from one network to another can require changing the configuration of all bridges on the internetwork.

A *learning* bridge, on the other hand, contains the intelligence to modify dynamically the address tables as each packet is handled. The locations of all stations in relation to the bridge location are also dynamically updated. A learning bridge can configure itself once the bridge knows its own address and where it fits in the internetwork.

A *router* (Fig. 1.16) is similar to a bridge except that it operates at the network layer (layer 3) of the OSI model. A bridge does not require any knowledge of the different protocols used by multiple LANs. A router, on the other hand, must know them. Routers work only with stations that use a common network layer protocol. Bridges generally operate faster than routers because they have fewer layers of software to process. Bridges are optimized for a few data link types and thus are cheaper. Routers, which are more expensive, must do more processing to forward messages because they sometimes include functions such as congestion control or message fragmentation and reassembly in addition to the transport functions. Message fragmentation and reassembly is required when stations on different networks accept packets of different sizes. Routers must contain the algorithms to read and translate many data link protocols. Routers are

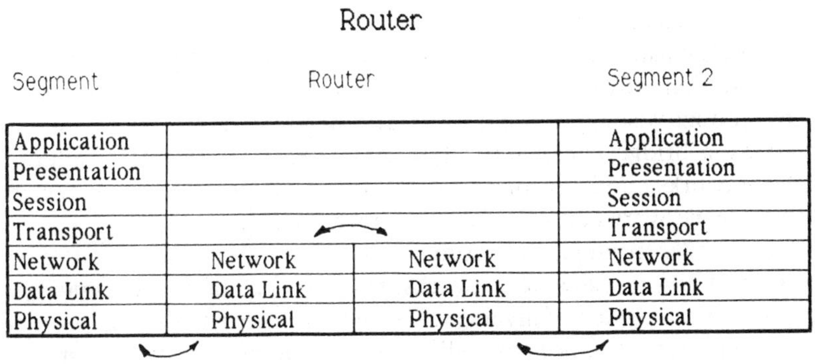

Router

Segment		Router	Segment 2

Application			Application
Presentation			Presentation
Session			Session
Transport			Transport
Network	Network	Network	Network
Data Link	Data Link	Data Link	Data Link
Physical	Physical	Physical	Physical

Figure 1.16 Routers operate at the network layer.

addressed directly by transmitting stations and therefore must have knowledge of the addresses and locations of all stations on all of the linked networks. Routers can use that knowledge of the network to choose the most direct routing for a given message between any two stations.

Routing can be static or dynamic. When static routing is used, all paths between networks are preset by the network manager. When dynamic routing is used, the router can learn new paths as changes occur. Static routing is not terribly desirable in a large network and can become very cumbersome if redundant message paths must be used.

Gateways (Fig. 1.17) are relays that connect two or more LANs with totally dissimilar protocols. A gateway must do protocol conversion for all seven layers of the OSI model, and generally operates from layer 3 (the network layer) up. A gateway acts as a protocol translator or interpreter between any two stations on the different networks and is usually used to construct global networks linking diverse local networks.

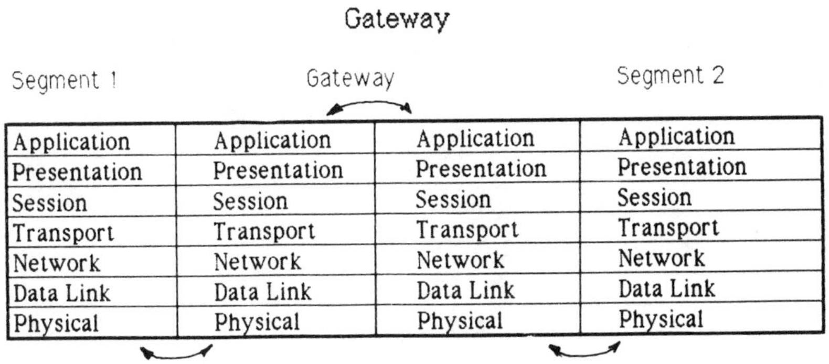

Gateway

Segment 1		Gateway	Segment 2

Application	Application	Application	Application
Presentation	Presentation	Presentation	Presentation
Session	Session	Session	Session
Transport	Transport	Transport	Transport
Network	Network	Network	Network
Data Link	Data Link	Data Link	Data Link
Physical	Physical	Physical	Physical

Figure 1.17 Gateways are complete protocol translators.

Communicating stations using one or more bridges are not aware of the bridge's existence. The bridge operates transparently to the communicating stations. Routers, on the other hand, must be addressed directly by any stations wishing to communicate through them. The cable segments served by a bridge are electrically independent, may connect heterogeneous networks, and are protocol-insensitive. Routers interconnect homogeneous networks and are protocol-specific (See Fig. 1.18).

Gateways, routers, and bridges are essential products for the construction of enterprise-wide networks, because such networks almost presuppose the connection of diverse LANs with different media and protocols over facility-wide distances as well as nationwide or worldwide distances.

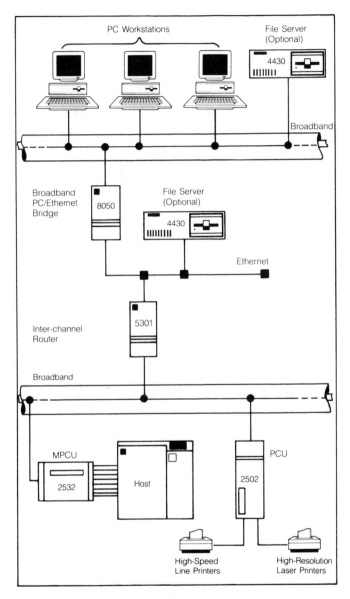

Figure 1.18 Routers are protocol specific. (Courtesy of Sytek.)

Chapter 2

Network Selection

The primary purpose of the LAN is to provide a flexible, integrated communication system that unifies an enterprise's data communications. In some cases, a LAN can unify data, video, and some voice services. Ideally, the network supports full connectivity for all users at the enterprise and allows each user to communicate with all other users. Typical supported applications might include electronic mail, word processing, access to shared data bases, spreadsheet applications, CAD/CAM/CAE, TV viewing, and process control or telemetry. If video applications are to be run, the media choices are limited to broadband and fiber. It is fair to assume that a typical broadband network will span multiple buildings at a single enterprise.

Especially at the enterprise level (all users at a single campus site or all users at campus and branch sites), the network should support multiple channels because there will probably be hundreds or thousands of users and some bandwidth-intensive applications. Batch downloads of large data bases and computer-aided design, manufacturing, or engineering require a large bandwidth.

It is important to estimate the amount of traffic that the network will be expected to support at various times of the day or during different times of the year. The type of traffic to be carried, the importance of the data carried, and the applications involved also make a difference. Process control data, which is real time, cannot safely be delayed. Data base access generally can tolerate some delay. Batch downloading of data bases, electronic mail, or file transfers, on the other hand, are relatively time-insensitive applications.

Among the key variables for throughput analysis is message size. Short, bursty messages are suitable for contention-based access protocols. Long batch downloads are best suited to very high speed networks or multiple-channel networks. The frequency of message transmission must also be considered. Infrequent messages mean light network loading, which can be handled by contention-based systems. Heavy loading and a requirement for determinate response is an argument for deterministic access protocols.

Here are a few rules that will help guide network selection. The key parameters include number of devices to be networked, typical device communication speed needed, bandwidth capacity of the carrying medium, maximum network distance to be covered, requirements for video or voice communication in addition to data, types of devices to be supported, and installation restrictions. In very general terms the choices can be broken down as PBX systems for voice and data systems operating at relatively low speed, baseband systems transporting data only at moderate to high speeds, and broadband systems transporting voice and video in addition to data at moderate to high speeds.

PBX networks generally use star topologies and twisted pair wire as a signaling medium. If modems or repeaters are not used, a digital PBX can transmit about 20 m. Data-only networks are supported by companies such as Develcon, Gandalf, and Micom. Supporters of integrated voice and data networks are GTE, AT&T, Mitel, Northern Telecom, NEC, Rolm, Siemens, Ericsson, Intercom, and Harris. The per port cost for a data-only network can vary from a few hundred dollars to more than a thousand dollars for an integrated voice-data approach. Generally speaking, top PBX systems will support asynchronous traffic up to about 19.2 kb/s. Some also offer connections to T-1 lines or X.25 networks. Links to host computers (other micros serving as file servers) also can be supported on many systems. Typical data transmission rates range from 300 to 9600 b/s. PBX networks are best suited to low-speed applications and conditions of light network loading.

Baseband networks are used most often in situations where the total number of ports is relatively small and where the dominant form of device connectivity desired is PC to PC. They offer high data transfer rates in situations where various forms of electronic mail, word processing, spreadsheet applications, and data base access are the major applications. Systems are available in speeds ranging from 2.4 to 56 kb/s, 10 Mb/s for Ethernet systems, and 50 Mb/s for Hyperchannel systems. For years, Proteon has had networks running at 80 Mb/s. Baseband systems are best for systems networking up to 100 devices. Baseband networks do not support video applications, and transmission distance is typically less than 20 km unless repeaters or bridges are used. ARCnet systems are available from numerous suppliers, including Novell. Ethernet systems are available from 3Com, Digital Equipment Corp. (DEC), Ungermann-Bass, Xerox, Excelan, Sytek, Novell, and many others.

Contention access systems such as CSMA/CD and CSMA/CA typically are best suited to baseband networks with network loading of 30% or less. As a general rule of thumb, token-passing access tends to work better when network loading exceeds 30%. Contention-based systems are better for asynchronous device communication, and are not as good for synchronous device communication at loading greater than 30%. Token passing tends to work well in scientific and engineering environments, process control and factory settings, and some office-automation applications where predictable access times are desirable. Token passing is not as efficient under conditions of light loading, however. Contention systems usually will offer faster access under conditions of light load.

3Com's EtherSeries line, Corvus Systems' Omninet, Datapoint's ARCnet, DECnet by Digital, Net/One by Ungermann-Bass, PCNet by Orchid Technology, and Nestar's ARCnet are some leading baseband networks. Datapoint and Nestar use token passing. The others use contention access.

Broadband systems generally operate up to 10 Mb/s per channel and are ideally suited to backbone network applications where high throughput is required and voice, video, and data services need to be supported. Broadband is advantageous where many hundreds to many thousands of users must be supported over campus-sized distances and where the form of communication includes video. Broadband is a good choice where network loading is very high. (At some point, fiber optic systems based on FDDI will become more important for high-speed backbone data transfer applications.)

Baseband bus networks (coaxial-cable-based) are usually a good choice for smaller networks with light to moderate traffic, and broadband bus networks are good for larger networks with heavy loading. System overhead tends to be relatively low for contention access systems and heavier for token-passing systems. Failure of a single station typically does not disrupt operations of the network, although a physical severing of the cable will cause a network crash on a bus network. Depending on where the cut is, a tree-structured broadband network will suffer partial outages on single or multiple legs. Only if the cable is cut soon after it comes out of the headend will a broadband network suffer a total network crash. Bus and tree networks are easy to expand or reconfigure.

Ring networks basically are a collection of point-to-point links and have the advantages and disadvantages of such links. No routing mechanism is required, and some ring networks can now transmit in both directions. Rings are a good choice where a small number of stations operating at high speeds over short distances is the operating environment. They are also good where a deterministic access system is preferred. The hardware part of the network is somewhat more complex, however, since every node on the network also functions as a repeater. Performance under heavy loading is relatively predictable, although average transmission delays will be long when the network is loaded lightly. Because a single break in the cable will crash the entire network, a redundant system is prudent. Costs to add another station to the ring are not high, although the network has to be brought down while the station is installed.

A popular way of getting around some of the single-point-of-failure and expansion issues is to go with a modified ring using wiring concentrators. This configuration strings together smaller star sections with bypass circuits. Thus, if one or more stations goes down, the entire ring stays operational. Only the stations connected to the one wiring concentrator would be affected.

The classic star network connects all workstations to a central switch and is the best way to integrate voice and data services at relatively low cost. Network performance depends on the power of the central processor, and overhead is high; therefore redundancy of the central processor is a good idea, because if the switch fails, the whole network crashes.

Media choices are a bit more complex than they used to be. In the past, users had their choice of twisted pair wire and baseband or broadband coaxial cable. Twisted pair was an inexpensive, simple way to link small numbers of workstations over fairly short distances at relatively low speeds at the risk of electrical interference. The low-speed characteristic will change soon as standards are set for Ethernet-speed connections over shielded twisted pair wire. The maximum throughput for a twisted pair network was about 1 Mb/s. Ethernet runs at 10 Mb/s.

The rules of thumb for coaxial cable remain pretty much the same. Baseband coaxial cable is suitable for small networks to networks of departmental size, supporting scores of terminals and extending a few thousand feet without repeaters. It is best suited to networks that are relatively lightly loaded with users that produce bursty traffic and relatively short messages. Baseband is not a medium for video or voice applications. Broadband still is suitable to larger networks with hundreds to thousands of users running a variety of applications, including video, bursty, and batch download traffic, and networked and point-to-point links running at a variety of speeds over distances as great as 12 mi.

Fiber optic systems have been relatively expensive until recently and have not offered much of a price-performance contest compared with broadband. Some specialty applications requiring high security or high immunity to RF and electromagnetic interference (military or factory) have been ideally suited for fiber networks. Still, the high cost of splitting and tapping fiber optic cable has made it a relatively unattractive choice for any user with a typical networking budget. That should change now that agreement on a very high speed token ring network, the FDDI, is almost complete.

As the demand for backbone networks and higher throughput has grown, a ring approach to fiber networks makes more sense. A ring is a collection of points, and point-to-point networks already are cost-effective (think of the long-distance telephone network). It appears FDDI will be an increasingly important standard for backbone networking of digital information over enterprise-type distances.

2.1 WORK-GROUP NETWORKS

Today, the typical number of nodes on a typical LAN is probably in the six to eight range. PC networking is the primary reason for that average number of ports. Even at large Fortune 500–sized firms, most of the networks are small work-group LANs. Here is an overview of a typical PC network.

Workstations, peripherals, a network operating system, and servers of various types are the building blocks of a PC LAN. Workstations almost always will be PCs of some sort. Servers are devices that primarily control access to the network, printers, and disk storage. The network operating system is software that typically runs on a PC, either dedicated or shared, that controls access to the various peripherals, and can be thought of as the disk operating system (DOS) of the network. The network operating system regulates user access to data, allocates disk space, and controls access to the printers. The operating system is used to assign passwords, restrict access to files, queue documents for access to printers, and run network diagnostics, for example. Dedicated servers are generally required when electronic mail or multiple hard disk access, larger numbers of users and faster access times are wanted. Nondedicated servers can be used when network loading is light and the numbers of workstations and network peripherals are small.

On many PC LANs a card called a *network interface unit* (NIU), containing the software and circuits to access the network, can be inserted into an empty slot in the PC. On broadband networks the NIU is typically an external unit containing RF modulation and demodulation circuits. The PC LAN NIU normally has a plug that mates to the cable or wire used to attach the PC to the network.

One of the most popular applications for LANs is data base access. On a single PC, data base access is not a problem. On a network, however, access is a major issue because many users may attempt to read the same data or to make changes to that data at the same time. *File locking* is one way to prevent multiple users from simultaneously altering the same record or file. File locking restricts file access to a single user at a time. *Record locking* is similar, but it restricts access to a particular record in a file to one user at a time. A variant of both file locking and record locking allows multiple users to read the same file or to record at the same time, but users cannot alter those files or records.

Control of access to disk space on a LAN is also important. On some simple LANs a common disk drive is partitioned into equal portions, and each user has access to his or her disk space but not to any others. Obviously, such a system is not suitable for data base access applications where many users must read or write common records.

Usually, common disks are managed as volumes with varying levels of access. A *public* volume permits access by all network users. Software that all users need, such as word processing, spreadsheets, or data base managers, would be in the public volume. These files typically are write-protected so that they cannot be accidentally altered. *Shared* volumes are available to a subset of users, but not to all users. Shared-volume users usually can read and write to files in the shared volume. *Private* volumes are restricted to the creator of the volume, and only the creator can read or write data to it. Subdirectories commonly are structured in each volume, and it is usually possible to restrict access on a read-write or read-only basis in each of the subdirectories, if desired.

A print server manages access to printers and can create a print queue on disk or buffer print orders. A spooler program is used to manage the flow of print orders.

Twisted pair, as we have said, is a good medium for point-to-point applications (rings and stars). Ethernet transmission speeds of 10 Mb/s are about to come onto the market, although low-speed and low-demand applications generally have been the arena for twisted pair networks. Twisted pair as a medium is easy to install and handle and is relatively inexpensive. Unshielded twisted pair is subject to electrical noise, however, and shielded twisted pair is a better bet.

Coaxial cable is generally used for broadband and baseband networks, when network distance is important (greater than twisted pair can handle, and possibly stretching to several miles), or for bus topologies. Various levels of immunity to electrical noise are offered by cable with different degrees of shielding, and installation costs are about the same as for twisted pair in most cases. Broadband coaxial cable is relatively bulky and harder to work with than ARCnet-type or Ethernet cabling, but it is relatively immune to high frequency noise. Low frequency noise, however, does cause problems.

Fiber optic cable offers high-speed throughput and immunity to RF and other electrical sources of noise (motors, arc welders, power lines). The cladding on most fiber optic cables offers protection similar to broadband-type coaxial cable. Currently, fiber is not very practical for topologies other than star networks because of the price of splitters and couplers required to run fiber in a bus or tree configuration. Fiber still works best as a point-to-point medium.

Ethernet is one of the oldest LAN protocols available, so it is not surprising that the base of Ethernet system vendors is large and influential. IBM intends to challenge the dominance of Ethernet with its token ring protocol, however, and looming on the horizon is the FDDI standard for backbone networks. Token-passing baseband and broadband bus systems like ARCnet and the MAP also will occupy important niches in the years ahead. International standards like the OSI model will grow in importance, and we can expect to see a gradual migration toward OSI standards by major vendors. At the subnetwork level, however, these proprietary standards will continue to be important because the investments companies have made in these technologies cannot be readily discarded.

Novell is a major vendor of several types of network architectures, including token ring, ARCnet (string of stars), bus, and star. However, Novell is a software house rather than a hardware vendor. Its proprietary NetWare operating system software is designed to run on any IBM PC or compatible machine and is compatible with networks sold by AT&T, Corvus, and 3Com. Novell can sell a customer a proprietary network, but, more importantly, it sells software or a software environment that runs on top of networks made by other vendors. NetWare has a justly deserved reputation for sophistication. The S-Net is a twisted pair star network supporting 24 workstations. Network components include a file server, disk storage, and controllers for up to five printers. The maximum cabling distance between a workstation and the file server is 1500 ft.

ARCnet is a distributed string-of-stars architecture that is similar, but not identical, to the IEEE 802.4 token passing bus standard. As many as 128 workstations can be supported by a single file server, and stations can be located as far away as 4000 ft from the file server. ARCnet systems use RG-62 coaxial cabling (it is the same cable used by IBM 3270 main frames). ARCnet uses token-passing access and both active repeater hubs and nonactive passive hubs. Drop cables from a passive hub can extend a maximum of 100 ft. Active hubs contain repeater circuitry and can send signals about 2000 ft if necessary. Network transmission speed is about 2.5 Mb/s.

For networks with faster throughput requirements, Novell has a licensing agreement with Proteon allowing NetWare to run on ProNET higher-speed networks. ProNET is a token passing string-of-stars topology with a throughput of 10 Mb/s. Wiring concentrators are available in 4-port, 8-port, or 12-port versions. If fiber optic cabling is used, the ProNET LAN can stretch as far as 1.5 mi. ProNET also runs on twisted pair and twinaxial cabling.

Novell also has a licensing agreement with Gateway Communications for use of NetWare on G-Net systems. G-Net is a 75-Ω coaxial cable bus network with a maximum network reach of 4000 ft. Transmission speed is rated at 1.43 Mb/s.

3Com, recently merged with Bridge Communications, also is a major LAN vendor, but has chosen to use a 10 Mb/s Ethernet-type 802.3 standard as its transmission protocol. Recently, the company has added 802.5 token ring standard access as well. Running on 50-Ω coaxial cable, a typical network can stretch about 3280 ft. When thin Ethernet cabling is used, transmission span shrinks to about 1000 ft. Multiple Ethernets may be linked by repeaters. The token ring version of 3Com's LAN is fully compatible with IBM's token ring network and runs at the required 4 Mb/s on shielded twisted pair wire.

AT&T offers several basic types of networks: StarLAN, Ethernet, and Information Systems Network (ISN). StarLAN is a relatively simple bus network linking up to 10 PCs using standard unshielded twisted pair telephone-type wire. The maximum reach of a StarLAN network is 400 ft. The 1-Mb/s system uses the CSMA/CD contention access system. The reach and number of nodes served on a StarLAN network can be extended by a two-tier approach to link as many as 100 workstations using a hub concept that clusters groups of workstations and links them with repeaters.

The higher-speed ISN integrates voice and data services in a star network using packet switching and a combination of fiber optic and twisted pair media known as the AT&T premises distribution system. Twisted pair is used to connect devices to packet controllers or concentrators. Fiber is used to link controllers up to 1 km apart. ISN will support both asynchronous and synchronous protocols. Operating at 8.64 Mb/s, ISN uses a unique access protocol that combines features of contention access that works best under lightly loaded conditions and token passing that works far better when a network is heavily loaded. Called *perfect scheduling,* the access protocol allows immediate access under light loads, as does Ethernet, but distributes access when the load gets heavy. AT&T also offers an Ethernet LAN.

Corvus makes the Omninet, a contention bus network operating at 1 Mb/s using twisted pair wiring and supporting as many as 64 workstations or nodes. The bus can extend up to 1000 ft or up to 4000 ft if repeaters are used. The Omninet hub system resembles the wiring closet design of

. StarLAN, supporting as many as 25 network branches from a single controller site. Each branch can support 10 workstations so long as total network nodes do not exceed 64. Multiple hubs can be used to extend network reach to 4000 ft. Access is by a contention-type CSMA protocol.

Apple Computer markets the AppleTalk Personal Network to support its Macintosh line of PCs. Although the network operates at low speed (about 230.4 kb/s) and to a maximum distance of about 1000 ft, it also offers a very low cost per connection, because interface circuitry is built into Macintosh and LaserWriter printers. Appletalk uses shielded twisted pair wiring and the CSMA/CA access protocol. AppleTalk networks are quite susceptible to high loading, though.

The IBM PC network is a broadband LAN supporting 72 IBM PCs, although compatible versions from other vendors will support over a thousand nodes. The PC network uses a CSMA/CD access protocol and operates at 2 Mb/s over standard CATV-type 75-Ω coaxial cable. Drop cables can run up to 200 ft, and maximum system distance can reach several miles. All software that runs on the PC network also will run on IBM's more strategic token ring network.

The token ring network runs at 4 Mb/s and supports up to 260 nodes using the IBM cabling system or up to 70 nodes using unshielded twisted pair wire. It conforms to IEEE 802.5 standards.

WangNet is a dual-cable broadband network offering nearly 400 MHz of bandwidth for transmissions in either downstream or upstream paths. It supports simultaneous channels of data, voice, and video. A modular user-installable version of WangNet is called FastLAN, which is recommended for small to medium-sized network applications. FastLAN uses the CSMA/CD access protocol, and data rates per channel are as high as 10 Mb/s. Other specified portions of the spectrum are set aside for dedicated 4.27-Mb/s, 2.5-Mb/s, 9600-b/s, and 64-kb/s service.

Apollo supports its computer products on the Domain network, a ring network using 75-Ω coaxial cable. The baseband system operates to about 1000 m and can support thousands of workstations or other devices at a maximum throughput of about 12 Mb/s.

3Com's Bridge Communications division supports both baseband and broadband networks using the Ethernet protocol on a variety of media, including broadband and baseband coaxial cable, fiber optic cable, or RG-62 ARCnet-type cable. Bridge uses the CSMA/CD access protocol, and maximum throughput is 10 Mb/s.

Concord Communications has a single-cable broadband network using token-passing access, running at 5 Mb/s and 10 Mb/s, and conforming to the 802.4 and MAP standards.

Contel supports baseband and broadband versions of its 802.3 standard ContelNet running in single- or dual-cable versions at 2 Mb/s and 10 Mb/s.

Datapoint developed ARCnet and continues to sell networks based on the token access string-of-stars topology that it pioneered in 1977. Datapoint networks operate at the standard 2.5-Mb/s throughput rate over RG-62 coaxial cable.

Digital Equipment Corporation was an early supporter of Ethernet, and its DECnet continues to be an important LAN medium. DECnet operates over broadband or baseband coaxial cable, fiber optic cable, or twisted pair wire and uses an 18-MHz channelization scheme.

Excelan's bus networks run on Ethernet-type coaxial cable and four-pair twisted pair wire at 10 Mb/s. Micom Systems also supports the Ethernet standard on coaxial cable and shielded twisted pair wiring. Xerox, the originator of Ethernet, runs its networks on baseband coaxial cable or four-pair twisted pair wire.

Allen-Bradley sells token-passing broadband networks to support its factory-automation equipment and supports the 802.4 and MAP standards.

Hyperchannel by Network Systems was the first really high speed network. It operates at 50 Mb/s on 75-Ω coaxial cable with the CSMA/CA access method and uses a bus typology.

Sytek was an early broadband LAN vendor and supports single-cable networks running on 75-Ω cable using the CSMA/CD access protocol.

Ungermann-Bass, one of the largest remaining independent LAN vendors, supplies baseband and broadband versions of its Net/One product line using broadband and Ethernet-type coaxial cable or fiber optic cabling. When a two-pair twisted pair standard for 802.3 protocol networks is adopted, the company will probably add a twisted pair version. Ungermann-Bass also supports token-passing broadband networks conforming to the 802.4 and MAP standards.

Applitek is a broadband network supplier with single-cable and dual-cable versions of its UniLINK network featuring either token passing or CSMA/CD access. Lanex offers both single-cable and dual-cable versions of its broadband network using the CSMA/CD access protocol. Zenith Electronics is the newest entrant in the broadband LAN market. Its Z-LAN system is a single-cable or dual-cable network that uses the CSMA/CD access protocol.

Chapter 3
The Basics of Broadband

A broadband network is an RF communication system that uses tree-type bus topology, standard CATV components, and runs on 75-Ω coaxial cable. The radio frequencies of interest on most broadband networks are those between about 7 and 450 MHz. In a general sense, broadband networks simply confine energy, similar to that used by TV broadcasters, inside a wireline transmission system, and, like TV broadcasters, broadband LAN users mix the desired signal (data, full motion video, or voice) with a higher-power RF carrier for transmission over metropolitan-sized distances.

A broadband LAN is especially useful for large networks because of its high bandwidth (337 MHz or more in each direction). (See Fig. 3.1.) The wider the bandwidth, the faster data can flow through the channel. The voice telephone network, for example, supports 3000 Hz, whereas a broadband system can handle 450 MHz or more. A digital PBX can support up to 100 simultaneous sessions. A broadband system can easily support scores of thousands of sessions.

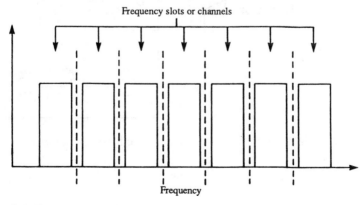

Figure 3.1 Frequency division multiplex (FDM).

Except for fiber optics, broadband is the only medium that can carry video, and it is one of the few media that can support thousands of users over distances as great as 30 mi and run many channels of video, voice, and data simultaneously.

A broadband network is a broadcast network. All messages bound from one station to another will pass all other devices on the network, although the devices will ignore the message if it is not addressed specifically to them. If security is needed, message encryption is possible. Consequently, broadband LANs allow easy device relocation and reconfiguration because broadband network addresses are properties of devices, not ports. If a device with a given address is moved from one port on the network to any other, the device need not be given a different address. As soon as it is plugged in, the device is operational. That is not the case with the public-switched telephone network or star topology LANs, for example, where the port, not the device, has the address. A telephone moved to a different outlet does not keep its telephone number, for example.

Broadband also is an ideal backbone medium for linking diverse departmental-sized networks together on a plantwide or campuswide basis. (See Fig. 3.2.) Broadband is one of the few LAN technologies capable of transporting signals for miles. It has the signal-carrying capacity to handle the hundreds or thousands of simultaneous data or voice communications that might occur on a very large campus-sized network. Broadband is the backbone network technology adopted by the IEEE 802 committee for MAC applications.

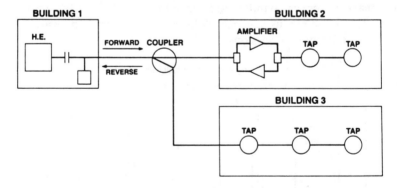

Figure 3.2 Broadband networks can span a facility-wide complex of buildings.

The technology also is quite robust: *mean times between failure* (MTBF) for active components typically run a minimum of 11 to 18 years. MTBF for passive components like taps can run 30–40 years.

Unlike unshielded twisted pair telephone wire, broadband has high immunity to RF and electromagnetic interference when cable plant integrity is high. Unterminated ports, cracked or damaged cable, loose connectors, or any improper maintenance will seriously degrade the broadband LAN network.

In addition, since a broadband system uses frequency division to separate the various channels it is running and does not use all of the bandwidth of the medium, it is possible to run several different networks simultaneously on a single cable, completely transparent to the users. A single cable can support, for example, a MAP network and an Ethernet system or a Sytek network and an Ethernet system.

Broadband probably is not the medium of choice for a small PC network in terms of either cost or capabilities. In this case broadband is overkill: it provides far more capacity than is required. If only a few data devices need to be connected and file transfers are small and relatively infrequent, a PBX approach, for example, makes sense. Broadband, however, is a must if video applications are required.

Although the commonsense wisdom of the past few years has been that broadband is more expensive than baseband (especially for very small PC networks), the price difference is not as great as in prior years. Many cost comparisons will show that a PBX LAN, for example, is more cost-effective than a broadband LAN. This is still true where the existing wiring can be used. But where hundreds of new connections need to be made, a PBX approach, which is assumed to use existing wiring, might cost as much as completely new broadband network. In short, baseband and broadband costs per connection are now very close where the number of connections is 500 or greater.

The actual data, video, and voice signals carried on the network are modulated (mixed) with an RF carrier that carries the signals to actual user ports on the network. Again, these RF carriers are the same as those used by over-the-air TV broadcasters to transmit TV programming. At each network terminal or node the RF carrier is stripped off by a modem and the actual signal is given to the receiving device. When a terminal wants to transmit, the opposite occurs: a signal ready for transmission is modulated with an RF carrier by the modem and then broadcast toward the network headend.

Broadband networks use frequency division to separate channels and thus can simultaneously transmit scores of video channels and hundreds of data channels. Perhaps without knowing it, users unfamiliar with broadband technology intuitively will understand how the many different signals transmitted on a single coaxial cable can avoid interference with each other. Consider an automobile radio tuner or a TV tuner. At any moment, all of the signals that are possible for either device to receive are bathing the receiver with energy, yet there is no interference between the various signals unless two transmitters are simultaneously using the same frequency. (For example, if you are listening to the radio while driving between cities, at some point the signal from one transmitter may begin to fade while the signal broadcasting from another city begins to come in stronger as the car gets closer to the transmitter site. For a while, the jumble of information from both transmitters may make both signals unintelligible.)

Broadband networks work the same way. So long as the various signals are separated by frequency, no interference results. As we will see later, it is possible to encounter interference produced by spurious signals and other harmonic artifacts produced by amplifiers or other active devices on a broadband network. In the main, however, RF networks avoid interference by separating signals by frequency and by using frequency-selective tuners to isolate a single channel at a time.

Broadband networks typically are channelized, or divided, into 6-MHz blocks. Recall that broadband is descended from CATV technology. A single TV channel occupies a 6-MHz bandwidth. The channel nomenclature generally used in the industry follows the conventions established by a joint committee of the National Cable Television Association (NCTA) and the EIA. Channels T7 through T13, running from 5.75 to 48 MHz, are known as the *sub-band*. The block from 54 to 88MHz is the *low band* and contains channels 2 through 6. The block from 108 to 174 MHz is the *midband*, channels 98, 99, and 14 through 22. Channels 7 to 13 occupy the block from 174 to 216 MHz and are known as the *highband*. The *superband* contains channels 23 to 36 and occupies frequencies from 216 through 300 MHz. The *hyperband* contains channels 37 through 94 and runs from 300 to 648 MHz. Most LANs will run from 5.75 through 400 or 450 MHz. (See Fig. 3.3.)

Within each 6-MHz block, multiple-data channels can be run. The amount of bandwidth depends on the speed required: the faster the transmission speed, the greater the bandwidth. As many as 56 data channels, requiring 96 kHz, can be run in a single 6-MHz channel. At 300 kHz per data carrier only 20 subchannels can be fitted into a single 6-MHz channel.

Frequency Allocation

TV CHANNELS

US & Canada

Chan	BW(MHz)	Pix	Color	Sound	Chan	BW(MHz)	Pix	Color	Sound
Sub-Band					**VHF-Super Band**				
T-7	5.75-11.75	7.00	10.58	11.50	J	216-222	217.25	220.83	221.75
T-8	11.75-17.75	13.00	16.58	17.50	K	222-228	223.25	226.83	227.75
T-9	17.75-23.75	19.00	22.58	23.50	L	228-234	229.25	232.83	233.75
T-10	23.75-29.75	25.00	28.58	29.50	M	234-240	235.25	238.83	239.75
T-11	29.75-35.75	31.00	34.58	35.50	N	240-246	241.25	244.83	245.75
T-12	35.75-41.75	37.00	40.58	41.50	O	246-252	247.25	250.83	251.75
T-13	41.75-47.75	43.00	46.58	47.50	P	252-258	253.25	256.83	257.75
					Q	258-264	259.25	262.83	263.75
VHF-Low Band					R	264-270	265.25	268.83	269.75
2	54-60	55.25	58.83	59.75	S	270-276	271.25	274.83	275.75
3	60-66	61.25	64.83	65.75	T	276-282	277.25	280.83	281.75
4	66-72	67.25	70.83	71.75	U	282-288	283.25	286.83	287.75
5	76-82	77.25	80.83	81.75	V	288-294	289.25	292.83	293.75
6	82-88	83.25	86.83	87.75	W	294-300	295.25	298.83	299.75
FM					**Hyperband**				
FM-1	88-94	89.25	92.83	93.75	AA	300-306	301.25	304.83	305.75
FM-2	94-100	95.25	98.83	99.75	BB	306-312	307.25	310.83	311.75
FM-3	100-106	101.25	104.83	105.75	CC	312-318	313.25	316.83	317.75
VHF-Mid Band					DD	318-324	319.25	322.83	323.75
A-2	108-114	109.25	112.83	113.75	EE	324-330	325.25	328.83	329.75
A-1	114-120	115.25	118.83	119.75	FF	330-336	331.25	334.83	335.75
A	120-126	121.25	124.83	125.75	GG	336-342	337.25	340.83	341.75
B	126-132	127.25	130.83	131.75	HH	342-348	343.25	346.83	347.75
C	132-138	133.25	136.83	137.75	II	348-354	349.25	352.83	353.75
D	138-144	139.25	142.83	143.75	JJ	354-360	355.25	358.83	359.75
E	144-150	145.25	148.83	149.75	KK	360-366	361.25	364.83	365.75
F	150-156	151.25	154.83	155.75	LL	366-372	367.25	370.83	371.75
G	156-162	157.25	160.83	161.75	MM	372-378	373.25	376.83	377.75
H	162-168	163.25	166.83	167.75	NN	378-384	379.25	382.83	383.75
I	168-174	169.25	172.83	173.75	OO	384-390	385.25	388.83	389.75
					PP	390-396	391.25	394.83	395.75
VHF-High Band					QQ	396-402	397.25	400.83	401.75
7	174-180	175.25	178.83	179.75	RR	402-408	403.25	406.83	407.75
8	180-186	181.25	184.83	185.75	SS	408-414	409.25	412.83	413.75
9	186-192	187.25	190.83	191.75	TT	414-420	415.25	418.83	419.75
10	192-198	193.25	196.83	197.75	UU	420-426	421.25	424.83	425.75
11	198-204	199.25	202.83	203.75	VV	426-432	427.25	430.83	431.75
12	204-210	205.25	208.83	209.75	WW	432-438	433.25	436.83	437.75
13	210-216	211.25	214.83	215.75					

Figure 3.3 Frequency allocation table. (Courtesy of Magnavox CATV.)

A rule of thumb for figuring bandwidth consumption at various data rates is to allocate 1 Hz for 1 b/s at 5 Mb/s and above, and about 2 Hz for each bit per second desired at lower rates. A transmission rate of 5 Mb/s, for example, can easily be handled by 6 MHz of bandwidth.

A single-cable broadband network not only divides frequencies between channels, much as a TV set might divide channels between 2 and 13, but it also divides the flow of signals by frequency. On a single-cable network, a portion of the spectrum is allocated for signals running from the headend out into the network. Another portion is reserved for signals returning to the headend from all other transmitter sites (modems and devices) on the network.

An early method for splitting signals is called *subsplit*. (See Fig. 3.4a.) On a subsplit network, the frequencies from 54 to 400 or 450 MHz are reserved for transmissions in the forward path—from the headend to all other sites on the network. The reverse, or return path, uses the frequency band from 5 to 30 MHz. The subsplit format is typically used by most CATV companies for separating forward and reverse paths.

A more popular system for LANs is called *midsplit*. (See Fig. 3.4b.) Midsplit offers a more equal division of channels and frequencies in the outbound and return directions. A typical midsplit system might use the bands from 168 to 400 or 450 MHz for forward path transmissions and the bands from 5 to 116 MHz for reverse path transmissions. The unused frequencies separating the forward and return paths are known as the *guard band*. (See Fig. 3.5.)

The newest method of frequency division is called *high split* or *equal split*. High split uses the bands from 232 to 400 or 450 MHz for the forward path and from 5 to 174 MHz for the reverse path.

Some broadband networks, however, use a dual-cable format rather than splitting frequencies for forward and reverse paths. One cable carries all signals outbound from the headend while a separate cable carries all signals inbound to the headend. Typically, a dual-cable network uses the band from 40 to 400 or 450 MHz for both inbound and outbound communications. Wang, TRW Information Networks, and Lanex are three vendors of dual-cable networks.

Why use a dual-cable network? Sometimes bandwidth (total information-carrying capacity) is very important. A dual-cable network doubles network capacity. Many large facilities will find that an existing base of different LAN technologies already in place puts a real premium on high bandwidth for facility-wide communications. It is not uncommon for large aerospace facilities to have numerous Ethernet, Wang, IBM, and DEC environment subnetworks already running. Linking those in-place networks can be a complex matter. Having 360 MHz available for both inbound and outbound paths tends to make frequency planning easier under such conditions.

Given that all devices on the network transmit only in a single direction (inbound toward the headend or outbound from the headend on either a single-cable or a dual-cable network), how is universal device connectivity maintained? It is maintained simply by frequency translation

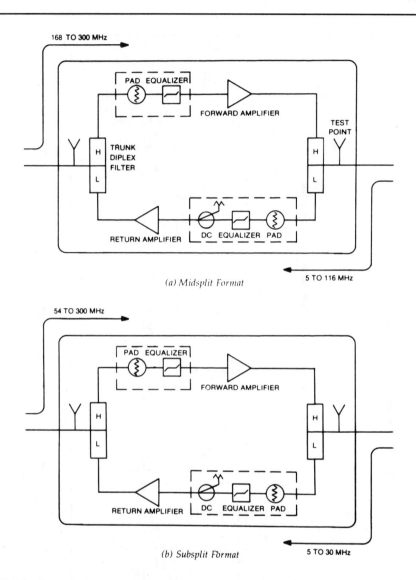

(a) Midsplit Format

(b) Subsplit Format

Figure 3.4 Typical two-way cable trunk amplifiers. (Courtesy of *CED.*)

58

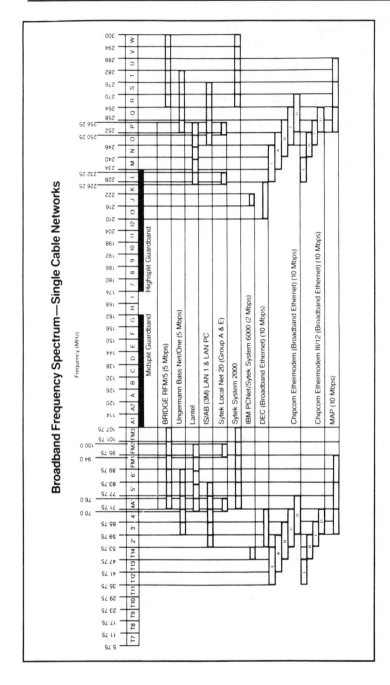

Figure 3.5 Broadband frequency spectrum—single cable networks. (Courtesy of Chipcom Corporation.)

at the headend (on single-cable networks) or by a simple loop-around connection at the headend (on dual-cable networks). (See Fig. 3.6.) On single-cable networks, two methods are commonly used for frequency conversion: simple frequency translation and remodulation. A *translator* is an electronic device that converts a block of frequencies from one range to another. A translator would take the inbound frequencies—from 252 to 288 MHz on a MAP network, for example—and change them into the lower frequencies used for the forward path. On a MAP network, the frequency band would be changed to the 59.75 to 95.75 MHz used for outbound transmissions.

A *remodulator* is similar to a translator in that it provides frequency translation from one set of frequencies to another. However, a remodulator provides better signal quality, especially noise performance by stripping away the RF carriers before the frequency translation occurs. In the process, all the accumulated noise generated as signals traveled through the network is removed with the RF carriers. The baseband data or analog signals are then remodulated, or mixed, with new RF carrier frequencies for the outbound trip. A headend remodulator can be thought of as performing the same functions as a modem: it strips away RF carriers so that the baseband, or actual, information can be read. Like a modem, a remodulator can impress an RF carrier on a digital signal.

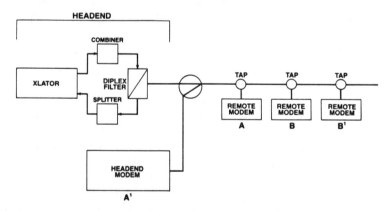

Figure 3.6 Frequency translation occurs at the headend.

Broadband networks are typically configured with a single master headend from which cable lines branch out much as a tree would. The headend usually is the place where frequency translation of inbound and outbound signals occurs and where network management and diagnostic consoles are located. If satellite signals are being received and transmitted on the LAN, the satellite receiving antenna and associated electronics would also be found at the headend. In addition, backup power sources and transmitters are often found at a headend. Sometimes, however, branch headends might be used to add redundancy to a system or to isolate network traffic within given buildings. A branch headend might be configured in such a way that traffic between stations or terminals in a single building stayed off the facility-wide network. Only those signals that are destined for terminals or stations elsewhere on the network might be permitted access to the backbone network by the branch headend.

A broadband LAN can use either a contention access protocol (normally CSMA/CD) or a token access protocol. Although structured physically like a tree, a token ring network, such as a MAP or IEEE 802.4 network, will logically function as a ring. The access token will be passed sequentially from one station to another as though the network were a physical ring.

3.1 BUILDING BLOCKS

The building blocks of a broadband LAN are the headend remodulator or translator, network monitoring and control system, the trunk and feeder system of cables, amplifiers, and power supplies to regenerate signals and transmit them over long distances, network interfaces (generally software embodied in a board-level product), and modems. (See Fig. 3.7.)

The headend is the central retransmission point for all signals carried on the network. On single-cable networks messages are carried toward the headend from all network nodes on what is called the reverse or return path. When they reach the headend, messages are translated to a higher set of frequencies for the trip outbound from the headend in the forward path.

You will hear the terms *translator* and *remodulator* used in connection with broadband LANs. A translator simply does frequency conversion, taking a block of frequencies and coverting it upward. A remodulator does the same thing, but it also demodulates the inbound signals—that is, it strips off the RF carriers—leaving the actual digital information or baseband video and voice signals. The signals are then remodulated (mixed with higher frequency RF carriers) for transmission outbound from the headend. In the process, packets are regenerated. The advantage of the remodulator as compared to the translator is that noise accumulated on the return path is removed from the signals before they are retransmitted.

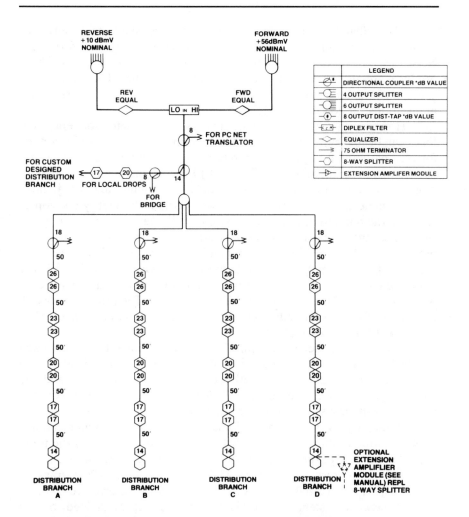

Figure 3.7 Basic broadband LAN. (Courtesy of Viewsonics.)

When dealing with point-to-point or multidrop modems designed to work on any general-purpose broadband network, you will sometimes see a specified translation offset. That offset refers to the number of megahertz that the inbound frequencies are upconverted before their outbound transmission.

Remodulators and translators are manufactured by C-COR Electronics, General Instrument's LAN Division, Catel Telecommunications,

Augat Broadband Engineering, and Viewsonics. All single-cable networks by Sytek, Ungermann-Bass, Concord Communications, TRW Information Networks, Lanex, or Applitek include translators or remodulators. These products are also available from distributors of broadband equipment, for example, Anixter Communications, Midwest Corporation, Merit Communications, or NCS Industries.

However, not all broadband networks use translators or remodulators. Dual-cable systems, which use one entire cable's bandwidth for the forward path and a physically separate cable for the reverse path, do not use frequency translation. (See Fig. 3.8.) Instead, the head end becomes a simple looping point where the outbound and inbound cables are joined.

A single-cable network requires some form of frequency division to separate the outbound, or forward, path from the reverse, or return, path. In essence, the entire signal spectrum of the cable (about 400 to 450 MHz) must be divided into three major bands: forward, guard, and reverse. Three common formats have traditionally been used to divide broadband system bandwidth. The subsplit format continues to be popular for one-way delivery of video signals by CATV companies. The return bandwidth is customarily set at 5 to 30 MHz while the forward band runs from 54 to 400 or 450 MHz. (See Fig. 3.9.)

On midsplit systems the return band is commonly set between 5 and 116 MHz while the forward band includes the 168 to 400 or 450 MHz. On high-split systems the reverse path often runs 5 to 174 MHz, and the forward path runs 232 to 400 or 450 MHz. Beyond this, however, the spectrum can be used in a variety of ways. For example, the MAP, a broadband-based LAN technology adapted for factory communications, specifies three channel pairs of 12 MHz each for its use. Any of the three pairs can be used to run MAP, leaving the rest of the spectrum open. The pairs are as follows: transmit 59.75–71.76, receive 252–264; transmit 71.75–83.75, receive 264–276; transmit 83.75–95.75, receive 276–288.

Broadband systems frequently are channelized, or divided, on the basis of standard TV channel assignments as used by the CATV industry. The CATV industry divides all bandwidth into 6-MHz blocks, each supporting one TV channel. The MAP channel pairs might be described, as transmit channels 3 and 4, receive channels P and Q; transmit channels A8 and 5, receive channels R and S; and transmit channels 6 and A5, receive channels T and U.

Network monitoring and control equipment are usually part of a broadband LAN headend. Network monitoring equipment measures channel use and data-frame distribution and keeps track of active network nodes. On a token ring network, the monitor keeps track of where the token is. Typically, monitors can keep track of transmission errors. Network analyzers inspect the actual data frames or packets being passed

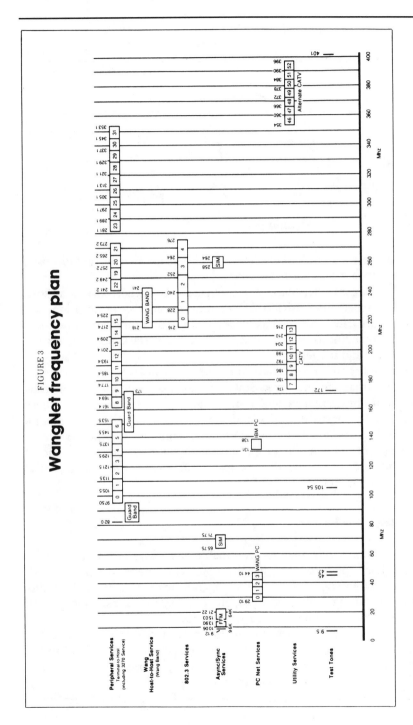

FIGURE 3

WangNet frequency plan

Figure 3.8 WangNet uses dual cable.

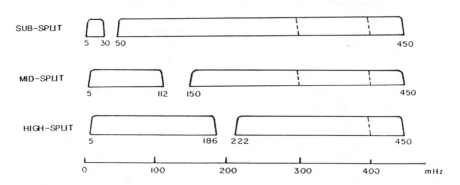

Figure 3.9 Frequency division plans.

around the network by stations. These analyzers are diagnostic tools used to debug software and hardware.

Network controllers can often configure network software, load software onto the network, provide alarm or out-of-tolerance notification, and provide security features such as assignment of passwords. Some network controllers function as network monitors and can track network errors, performance, and usage.

Network monitors are concerned with the data transport or "digital" portion of a broadband network. Status monitoring systems also keep track of the status of amplifiers and power supplies on the network. These systems usually consist of a headend controller and transponder units located at various points on the network (every amplifier and power supply location, every other amplifier and power supply location, at the end of each trunk or distribution cable, or just at the end of trunks with critical traffic moving on them).

3.1.1 Status Monitoring

Status monitoring systems are capable of tracking ac line voltage, dc battery voltage, pilot carriers (usually a high carrier and low carrier), RF signal strength, amplifier or power supply housing temperature, humidity transponder current draw, housing open or shut status, transponder output level, and active condition of bridger switches.

Status monitoring systems provide alarm or out-of-tolerance notification to the console operator and isolate the position of the fault to the nearest amplifier or cable span. (See Fig. 3.10.) Alarm windows are frequently user-definable. Transponders might be set, for example, to report any increase or decrease in signal level 1.5 dB or greater. Some status

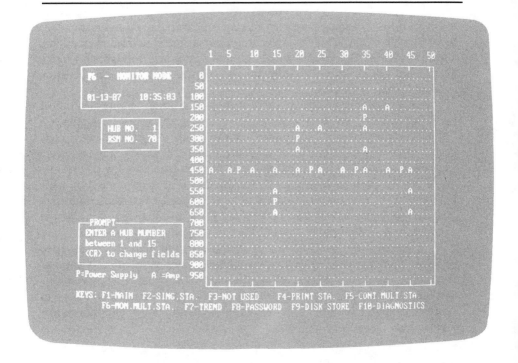

Figure 3.10 Status monitoring software.

monitoring systems will report and display on the console monitor all changes of signal level within a few tenths of a decibel. Others simply report that a station is within tolerance or not within tolerance.

Although status monitoring is important for locating catastrophic problems, it is perhaps more useful as an early warning system because broadband systems tend not to fail catastrophically but to drift slowly out of compliance. If moisture began accumulating at any point between two amplifiers, for example, the attenuation between those amplifiers, would gradually increase and automatically trigger compensation by each amplifier's internal *automatic gain control* (AGC) circuits, which would increase power draw to both amplifiers.

Regular observation of the normal status of the amplifiers and power supplies on a network would quickly tip off an operator to possible problems when the normal power consumption indices began to drift higher, for example. Some status monitoring systems also offer statistical features that can simplify network management. Magnavox's Digital Sentry System (DSS) can store information on particular faults, so a systemwide index can be built over time. Say that amplifiers on a network tend to get an average of four warning messages a year. Any amplifier that gets 20 needs to be checked. The DSS system can monitor as many as 16,368 locations, and the software displays information on temperature, voltage, and signal level in bar graph form. The software also has routines that help operators localize ingress locations.

Some systems on the market, such as Scientific-Atlanta's, monitor two pilot carriers, one at a high frequency and one at a low frequency. C-COR Electronics has a system that measures only a high frequency pilot, because the signal attenuation is greatest there. The Magnavox system watches two pilots, one outbound and one return, as does the system marketed by General Instrument's Jerrold division. A newer system marketed by AM Communications sweeps all frequencies in steps, rather than just the pilot carriers. It also is designed to be used at any point on the network, not just amplifier, end-of-line, or power supply locations.

Many of the status monitoring systems on the market are designed to work with a particular vendor's amplifiers. Texscan Communications' system, however, was designed from the start to function with any vendor's amplifiers. Generally speaking, interfaces to the common standby power supplies available on the market are supplied by the power supply vendors themselves.

3.1.2 Cable

Broadband LAN trunk cables range from 0.412 to 1.000 in in diameter; cables 0.500 in or larger are usually used for LAN trunks. Feeder cables commonly are jacketed or unjacketed 0.500-in aluminum. Drop cables typically are RG-11, RG-6, or RG-59 and have foil and braid shielding to prevent egress or ingress of RF energy. Keep in mind that current National Electrical Code (NEC) rules recommend the use of flame-retardant and low-smoke-producing jackets, such as Teflon or conduit, for plenum or riser applications inside buildings. Actual regulations will vary from locality to locality and are subject to the local electrical inspector's interpretation of those codes.

Trunk cables are available in five categories. Plain cables have no polyvinyl chloride (PVC) jacketing over the aluminum sheath. Jacketed cables add a PVC layer for protection. Jacketed cables designed for earth burial have a flooding compound to reject moisture. For aerial applications, an integral support (messenger) cable is added. When ruggedness is a primary concern, armored and jacketed cables are available, as is a new type of cable developed by General Instrument's Comm/Scope Division.

Called Cable Guard, it combines the crush-resisting properties and cut-through resistance of traditional armored cable with the greater flexibility, easier connecting, lighter weight, and smaller bend radius of standard jacketed cable.

Most trunk cables use foam as a dielectric. Trilogy Communications, however, uses air as the dielectric material. Capscan, a division of Burnup & Sims, Times Fiber Communications, and General Instrument Network Cabling Division manufacture trunk, feeder, and drop cables. Trilogy makes trunk and feeder cable, and Belden specializes in drop cabling.

The bending radius of unarmored foam dielectric trunk cables ranges from about 6 to 14 in. Armored versions will run between 9 and 17 in. Air dielectric cable, which is insensitive to the effects of armoring and jacketing, has a bending radius from 5 to 13 in. The velocity of propagation for foam cabling is about 87%. Air dielectric provides about 93%.

Drop cable specifications normally include provisions for a high degree of shielding to prevent signal ingress or egress. Basically, four types of drop shielding are used: braids, laminate foil tapes with a braid on one side of the tape, laminate foil tape with a sheath on both sides of the tape, and what Times Fiber calls Quadshield (a tape-braid-tape-braid shielding).

Transfer impedance, one measure of shielding effectiveness, relates a current on one surface of the shield to the voltage drop generated by this current on the opposite side of the shield: the lower the impedance value, the better the shielding. At 100 MHz, for example, values can run between 48 and 0.1 mΩ/m. RG-59 cable with a 96% braid, at 300 MHz, has a transfer impedance about 1000 times greater than a cable with 60% sealed foil and 40% braid foil, according to Times Fiber.

The quality of shielding is especially important as frequency increases from 300 to 400 MHz, because shielding effectiveness decreases as frequency increases. Times Fiber once conducted a study on outdoor drop cables, some of which had been in continuous use for 23 years. The most significant aging effect noticed was a deterioration of shielding effectiveness. Foil-braid-foil had the lowest leakage and the best shielding performance.

Center conductor materials typically are copper-clad aluminum, although solid copper conductors are available. Above 5 MHz, both exhibit equal electrical properties. Copper-clad aluminum is lighter, cheaper, and has better *structural return loss* (SRL) characteristics, though. Times Fiber uses both copper-clad aluminum and copper-clad steel in its cables.

General Instrument's Network Cable Division is a major manufacturer of 75-, 50-, 93-, and 100-Ω cabling in four major categories. Its RG specification cables are based on modified military specifications (Mil-

Spec). Its commercial cables use reduced braid. Its Mil-Spec cables are made to full military standards, but are not fully QPL (qualified products list) tested. The Mil-Spec cables meet all government QPL standards.

Network Cable Division's sister company, Comm/Scope, specializes in trunk and feeder cable. Drop products come in plenum and standard, single, and dual (two drops connected by a web) versions. Trunk cables come in jacketed and unjacketed versions in 0.500- and 0.750-in versions, both armored and nonarmored. Also new is the Cable Guard jacketed cable, a compromise between armored and plain jacket cables. Drop cable comes in braid, foil-braid, Trishield, and Quadshield construction and in RG-59, RG-6, RG-11, and video broadcast versions. Special corrosion-resistant or armored trunk and feeder cables are also made by the company.

Network Cabling Division also is emphasizing MAP and TOP applications for its cabling, recommending in particular RG-6 and RG-11 specification cables for MAP or TOP networks. Quad RG-6 and plenum quad RG-6, as well as quad RG-11, plenum quad RG-11, and armored quad RG-11 are available. These cables use copper-clad steel-center conductors, quad shielding, and meet all industry crush, twist, and bend standards. Phase delay distortion and transfer impedance requirements of the MAP 802.4 specification are met.

Times Fiber Communications makes three families of cable. The T-4 family of trunk and feeder cables runs from 0.412 to 1.000 in; the drop series includes RG-59, RG-6, RB-611, RG-11, and headend cable, and plenum drop cables (59, 6, and 11). The TX series is designed for very low loss applications and includes 0.565, 0.840, and 1.160 cables in jacketed, jacketed and flooded, and armored versions. There also is a jacketed and messengered version in 0.565 cables.

T-4 trunk and feeder cables are available in aluminum sheath, jacketed, jacketed and messengered (0.412, 0.500, and 0.625 in), jacketed for burial, and jacketed and armored versions.

The RG-59 and RG-6 standard and premium drop cables use foil and braid shielding. The Trishield versions use tape-braid-tape construction. The Quadshield versions use tape-braid-tape-braid construction. The 611 and 11 series of drop cables come in two versions: standard with foil-braid shielding and Quadshield. Single, messengered, flooded, Siamese (two cables attached by a web), and Siamese messengered (two cables attached by a web and including a messenger) versions are available. The Siamese versions are particularly good for dual-cable plant. A new moisture-resistant cable, lifeTime, also is available.

Capscan, a division of Burnup & Sims, has a coaxial cable (CC) line of super low loss trunk cables, available in aluminum sheath, jacketed, jacketed for burial, jacketed and messengered, or jacketed and armored versions from 0.412 to 1.000 in. The company's drop cable line comes in two major families: coaxial drop and Quadshield. The coaxial drop line uses a tape-braid shielding. The Quadshield uses tape-braid-tape-braid. A variety of foam densities are available: 59, 6, 7000, and 11.

Belden specializes in drop and network cables of every sort: fiber optic, Ethernet, AppleTalk, triaxial, twinaxial, CB, audio, ribbon cable, instrumentation, RS-232, RS-422, RS-423, RS-485, and Mil-Spec. For broadband applications, the company is known for its high-quality drop cables. Belden uses a foil-braid-foil construction with a shorting fold in the outermost foil to provide better transfer impedance performance than some four-layer shields do. In addition, Belden bonds the inner foil to the jacket, making it easier to strip and connector the cable. SRL testing, a measurement of cable integrity, normally is done to cabling prior to shipping, typically over the entire 5–450 MHz bandwidth. Desired specs are a minimum of 23-dB return loss for RG-59 and 26 dB for RG-6 cables. Belden's RG-6 and RG-59 drop cables come in messengered, nonmessengered, dual, and flooded versions. Also available are bundled cables (eight drops in a single jacket), headend cable with a silver-plated center conductor, and direct-burial cable.

Trilogy Communications specializes in trunk and distribution cables using air dielectric. Its MC2 line runs from 0.440 to 1.000 in in diameter and offers both solid copper and copper-clad aluminum center conductors. Trilogy's cables come in aluminum sheath, jacketed aerial, jacketed direct-burial, messengered, and armored versions. New from the company is a 0.500-in plenum cable, the Fused Disc MIII, meeting NEC guidelines for flame and smoke retardance.

3.1.3 Amplifiers

Amplifiers (see Fig. 3.11) repeat and strengthen the amplitude of signals transmitted on a broadband network. Amplifiers are necessary because RF signals attenuate, or lose strength, as they pass through coaxial cable, connectors, taps, splitters, and other portions of the distribution system. A variety of amplifiers, or main stations, are used on broadband networks. Trunk amplifiers are used on the backbone cabling system and are generally designed to accept a low input signal level (10 to 12 dBmV, for example) and add 20 to 28 dB of gain so that the output level is between 32 and 34 dBmV. Since many amplifiers may be linked serially, or cascaded, on a broadband trunk, and since every amplifier circuit will introduce some level of distortion and noise as it boosts signals, trunk amplifier design philosophy emphasizes low distortion. (See Fig. 3.12.) Low distortion is achieved in part by limiting the degree of gain at any single amplifier

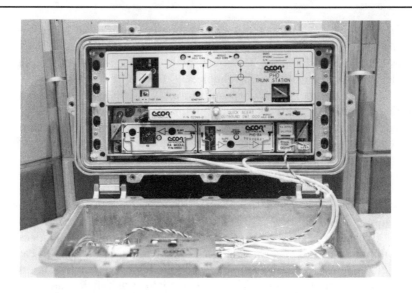

Figure 3.11 Broadband amplifier

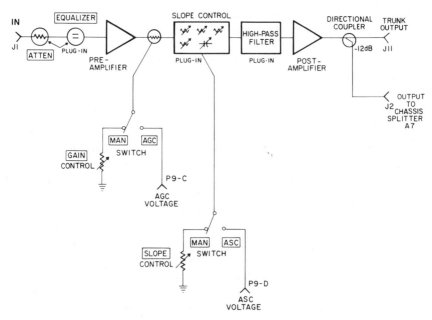

Figure 3.12 Trunk amplifier functional block diagram. (Courtesy of Magnavox CATV.)

location: the lower the gain, the lower the distortion. However, the trunk amplifiers will contribute most of the noise in a broadband system.

Bridger amplifiers are used to tap RF energy off a trunk line for distribution to a feeder network. (See Fig. 3.13.) The bridger amplifier is designed to run at high gain, 47 to 50 dBmV. Because it is operated at high gain, the bridger will produce relatively more distortion than will a trunk amplifier. For this reason, bridger amplifiers typically are followed by no more than two or three line extenders.

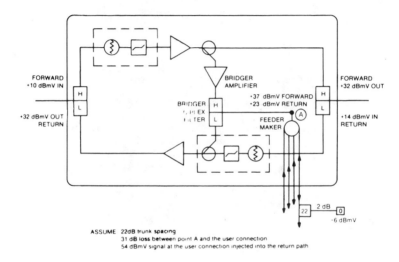

Figure 3.13 Trunk and bridging amplifier. (Courtesy of *CED*.)

Line extenders (LEs) are lower-cost amplifiers with higher distortion and noise figure specifications than trunk or bridger amplifiers have. LEs are physically smaller than trunk amplifiers and are designed to accept higher input signal levels, 20 dBmV or so. (See Fig. 3.14.) They also contribute more noise and more distortion to amplified signals than trunk amplifiers do, but they consume less power. LEs are not designed to accept AGC or ASC modules or to be cascaded. When two LEs are used serially, they are usually run at about 3 dB less gain than if each were operating alone. (See Fig. 3.15.)

Internal distribution amplifiers are high-gain units often used in high-rise office buildings or other large facilities where feeders must run over several floors. They typically contain their own internal power supplies and do not draw ac current from the cable itself.

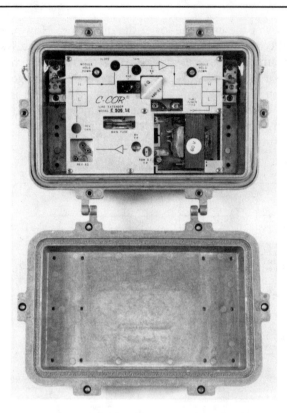

Figure 3.14 Line extender housing.

Broadband amplifiers normally are housed in watertight aluminum housings that reject moisture and prevent signal ingress or egress. (See Fig. 3.16.) In addition to the actual gain circuits, amplifiers usually have equalizing circuits that are designed to compensate for the uneven attenuation experienced by RF signals as they move through coaxial cable. Higher frequencies attenuate more than lower frequencies. Equalizers compensate for this differential attenuation to produce a flat signal amplitude to the gain circuits before amplification occurs. (See Fig. 3.17.)

Sometimes (for example, when an amplifier is short-spaced) signal levels must be attenuated at the input of the gain stage. A *pad,* or *attenuator* (see Fig. 3.18), does this. Pads normally are available in values of 0, 3, 6, 9, and 12 dB.

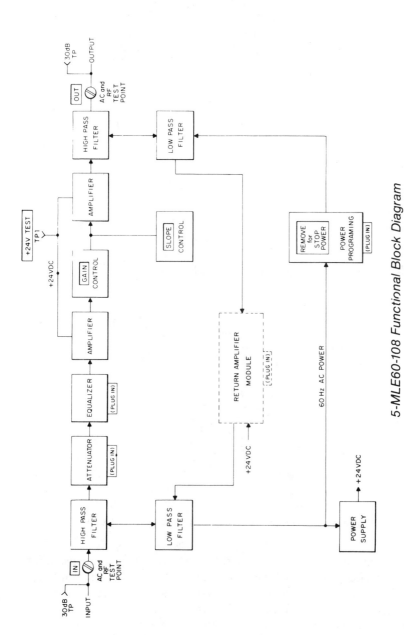

Figure 3.15 Line extender. (Courtesy of Magnavox CATV.)

5-MLE60-108 Functional Block Diagram

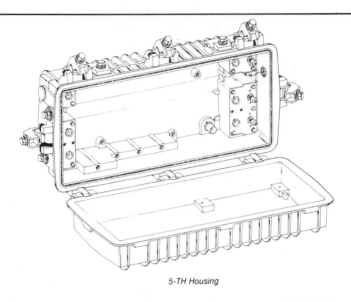

5-TH Housing

Figure 3.16 Amplifier housing. (Courtesy of Magnavox CATV.)

5-CE 440 A *

Figure 3.17 Common equalizer. (Courtesy of Magnavox CATV.)

Additional circuits that regulate the gain circuits and compensate for temperature effects also are commonly found within a main-station housing. AGC circuits sense actual input signal levels and can raise or lower amplifier gain accordingly. If the AGC senses that input level is 1 dB low, then gain is boosted by 1 dB to compensate. A more precise form of AGC is *automatic slope control* (ASC). An AGC circuit will raise or lower signal

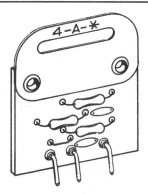

Figure 3.18 Attenuator. (Courtesy of Magnavox CATV.)

levels by the same amount across the entire passband. Recall that higher frequency signals attenuate more than lower frequency signals. So even if initial signal level is flat across the entire passband, it will not be flat after passage through a single span of cable. At the input of the second amplifier, the signal levels of lower frequencies will be relatively stronger than the signal levels of higher frequencies.

A plot of signal level *versus* frequency is a diagonal line. This line is called the *slope*. ASC circuits have the ability to boost signals differentially: more gain at higher frequencies, less gain at lower frequencies. Equalizers compensate for slope.

Amplifier housings contain 60-V power supplies that take ac from the cable and change it to 24 V dc for actual use by the amplifier modules (see Fig. 3.19) and status-monitoring transponders. A status monitoring system is a network management and control tool consisting of software, a headend controller, and device telemetry stations usually positioned at amplifier and power supply locations and end-of-line cable runs. See Section 3.1.1.

Status monitoring systems sometimes allow remote triggering of A/ B switches, which allow the network to default to a redundant cable path if the main path fails. (See Fig. 3.20.) Some systems permit remote triggering of three-position bridger switches that can selectively isolate legs of the network for fault isolation.

Amplifiers also contain various filters to separate reverse path and forward path signals as they pass through the amplifier circuits. (See Fig. 3.21.) Systems using pilot carriers on the reverse path (transmitting from the ends of trunks toward the head end) require reverse path, pilot carrier generator modules and return carrier filters.

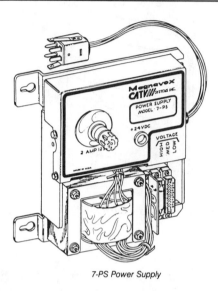

7-PS Power Supply

Figure 3.19 Amplifiers use internal power supplies to convert ac to dc. (Courtesy of Magnavox CATV.)

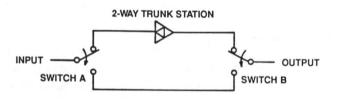

Figure 3.20 Passive redundancy switch.

CATV systems routinely use subsplit amplifiers, which allocate nearly all their bandwidth to carry video signals to subscribers (54 to 400 or 450 MHz out, 5 to 30 MHz return). In a LAN environment, much more bandwidth is necessary on the return path. Two methods are commonly used. Dual-cable systems dedicate an entire cable for inbound transmissions and a separate cable for outbound transmissions. Single-cable systems achieve better frequency allocation by using the midsplit (typically 168 to 400 MHz forward, 5 to 116 MHz return) or high split (232 to 400 MHz out, 5 to 174 MHz return) formats.

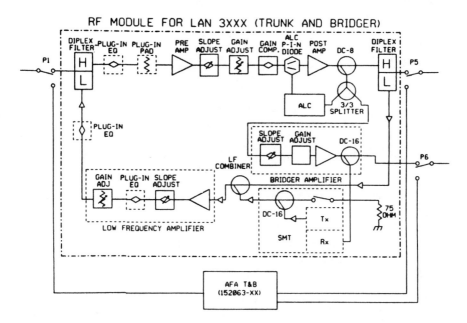

Figure 3.21 Amplifiers use filter circuits. (Courtesy of C-COR Electronics, Inc.)

Chapter 4
Components

The physical distribution system used by a broadband network has several major parts. The headend is the common point of communication for all ports on the network and serves as a central broadcast point for all outbound messages. (See Fig. 4.1.) The headend normally contains such equipment as frequency translation or remodulation gear, power supplies (both primary and backup), combining and filtering circuits, and network management and control consoles. Status monitoring consoles for the distribution system are also usually located at the headend. Gateways to dissimilar networks on the same premises or bridges to other broadband networks or network segments would be located at the headend. If satellite communication links a broadband network with other sites, the headend will typically contain all the signal processing equipment associated with the earth station or stations: antennas, receivers, frequency down-converters, demodulators, and modulators. If a microwave link is involved, the headend will also house antennas, receivers, and transmitters.

Radiating out from the headend in a branching function is the network of trunk and distribution cables that carry signals out to network user sites. (See Fig. 4.2.) On the trunk system are amplifiers to regenerate signal strength, transponders to monitor distribution system performance, and power supplies for the amplifiers and other active devices. Passive, nonpowered devices such as couplers and splitters will be inserted into the cable at periodic intervals to remove signals for distribution to the feeder system. Rarely will actual user ports be located immediately off a trunk cable. Most often, user taps are cut into the distribution and feeder cables that branch off the main trunk lines.

Feeder or distribution cable segments serve *taps* (see Fig. 4.3), devices that remove a small portion of energy on the cable for delivery to one port or to multiple-user ports. A length of drop cable not more than 100 f generally runs from the tap to the wallplate, to which a device is

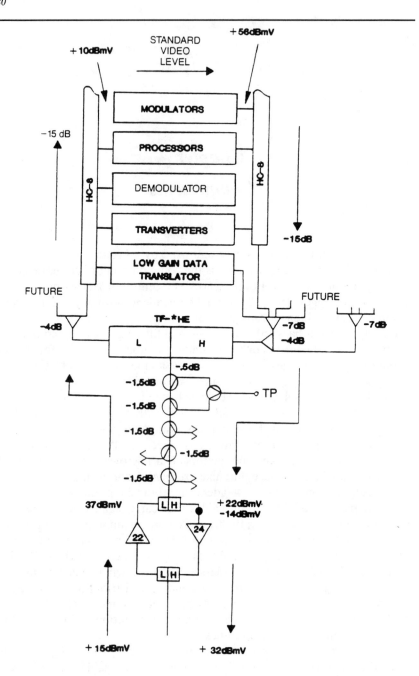

Figure 4.1 Standard broadband headend. (Courtesy of General Instrument Corporation.)

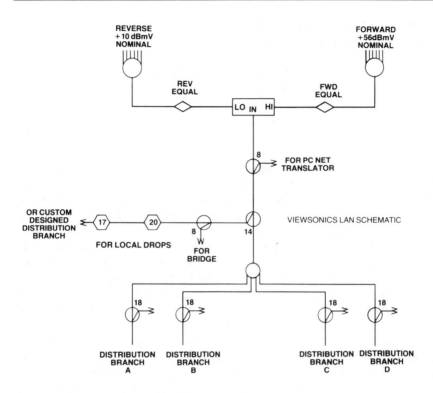

Figure 4.2 Headend schematic.

Figure 4.3 Tap.

attached. All devices connected directly to the network need a modem to strip off the RF carrier energy, read messages, and modulate outbound messages with the assigned RF carrier.

Amplifiers and signal effects associated with amplifiers probably account for most of the design, operational, and maintenance issues a broadband LAN user will face. For this reason we will pay heavy attention to amplifiers and the effects amplifiers have on signal transmission. The properties of coaxial cable, power supplies, and passives (taps, couplers, splitters) will be examined. The headend is probably the best place to start.

The headend is the single point of network failure and the place where much of the diagnostic equipment and network monitoring take place. First, we look at some of the equipment that can be used to communicate with other networks, such as satellite and microwave systems. Satellite communication as it pertains to the LAN environment is largely a matter of reception, not transmission. That is, most users want a system that can receive signals rather than transmit them. Although it has not been the primary focus of most broadband LANs, video signal distribution should, over time, become a more important mix of network traffic. For this reason we look briefly at how over-the-air TV signals can be imported and distributed on a broadband network.

Microwave links are increasingly important gateways to telephone company points of presence, linking LANs with the wider public telephone network. Traditionally, most broadband technology users have been CATV operators, who used microwave frequencies in the 13- and 18-GHz ranges. Private point-to-point links are commercially available at 23 GHz, but the principles of signal transportation and processing are the same.

We next examine the equipment used to modulate signals for transmission through the actual cable network itself. Of the devices involved, the modulator, which mixes an RF carrier with baseband signals, the translator (see Fig. 4.4), which converts a block of frequencies from one range to another, and the remodulator, which demodulates inbound signals and then remodulates them for outbound travel, are the most important.

Bridges, gateways, and routers are also important headend devices. They will be described in the next chapter, along with modems.

Headend equipment has several functions. For communication with other networks (by microwave link or satellite, for example), there are pairs of modulation and demodulation circuits, receivers, transmitters, associated signal combining circuits, receiving and transmitting antennas, and frequency down-conversion and up-conversion devices that change the frequencies from the megahertz range to the gigahertz range used by satellites and microwave transmission systems.

Signal processors, on the other hand, are used to receive off-air TV broadcasts. The input to a signal processor comes from a TV antenna.

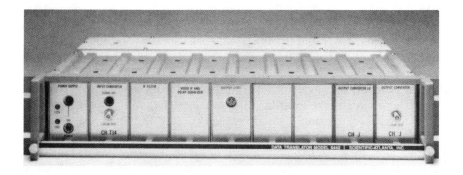

Figure 4.4 Data translator. (Courtesy of Scientific-Atlanta.)

Any frequencies aside from those desired are rejected at the input by filters. Each 6-MHz channel requires its own signal processor, although the processor itself may be *frequency agile*; (that is, the processor is capable of being tuned to receive different frequencies rather than only one fixed frequency). Off-air signals are down-converted to an *intermediate* frequency (IF) and then amplified. Then the video and audio signals are separately amplified again and recombined. The signal is then up-converted to the desired frequency for transportation on the network. That frequency can be the same as originally received or any other frequency to about 600 MHz.

Generally, at the headend all received video and audio signals are amplified, adjusted for signal level to make all levels on the network identical, maintained at a constant output level, and frequency converted. Signals also must be combined before leaving the headend, and pilot carriers, sometimes used as reference signals for the AGC and ASC circuits in amplifiers, must be inserted.

For communication to all internal points on the network there are modulators, remodulators, or translators to add RF carriers to baseband signals. Filtering circuits and combining circuits are generally used at the headend for managing internal communications.

4.1 MICROWAVE LINKS

Both single-channel and multichannel technologies are available for microwave links, and *frequency modulation* (FM) and *amplitude modulation* (AM) formats are routinely used. FM offers better noise performance but at the cost of additional bandwidth (between two and four times the bandwidth per channel required by AM techniques). If a single-channel

FM technique is used, an RF transmitter and receiver are required for each 6-MHz channel, assuming communication is bidirectional between the broadband LAN and the other network. Signals transmitted over the microwave link also must be amplitude modulated after being transmitted by the FM format, so modulation and demodulation circuits are required for the AM-to-FM conversion and FM-to-AM reconversion at the receiving site. These circuits are located in the transmitters and receivers.

Some FM transmitters and receivers accept IF inputs, usually at 70 MHz. IF inputs are simply lower frequency versions of the microwave carrier, and they offer the advantage of longer transmission distance because of better distortion performance. Equipment accepting the IF input is known as *heterodyne* and works on the principle of frequency conversion only. There is no actual demodulation of this signal. In a heterodyne process, two frequencies are mixed to produce a different frequency. FM equipment requiring remodulation of AM signals is known as a remodulating system, a baseband system, or an FM system. At the receiving site or sites, as well as at any intermediate repeater sites, the incoming microwave signal is received, mixed with a local oscillator reference, and then down-converted to an intermediate frequency, which is amplified and demodulated. The signal is then again remodulated, amplified, and transmitted to the next station. Each modulation and demodulation stage will add some distortion.

If a multichannel AM format is chosen for the microwave link, things are simpler. AM microwave systems do not require the modulation and demodulation process that converts AM to FM to AM. Instead, AM transmitters can accept standard RF carriers at their input. In effect, the AM transmitter is a frequency up-converter that produces a microwave carrier in the gigahertz range, rather than lower-power, megahertz-range broadband RF carriers. Both low-power and high-power AM systems have commonly been used by CATV operators. The low-power variant uses a maximum of eight RF carriers. If more than eight channels must be transported, an additional transmitter is used. The high-power variant assigns a single RF transmitter to each microwave channel.

The range of microwave frequencies runs from about 900 MHz to 20 GHz, and those frequencies traditionally used by CATV and private operators such as school systems and churches have been from 12.7 to 13.2 GHz. An additional set of frequencies at about 18 GHz has also been alloted for CATV use. Common carrier microwave frequencies have been set aside at roughly 4, 6, 11–12 and 13 GHz. Common path distances range from 5 to 25 mi.

Microwave antennas are highly directive and have high gain: the higher the frequency used or the larger the diameter of the antenna, the higher the gain. An antenna about 6 ft in diameter has a gain figure of 40 dB or more. Most antennas are made of aluminum, and some are fiberglass. The antennas are always mounted in a direct line-of-sight location. Waveguides are used to direct signals from the antenna to transmitters or receivers. Rigid, rectangular, tube-type guides are used in the headend. A semiflexible version is commonly used for actual connections to the antenna. Where less attenuation is desired, a circular waveguide can be used.

The test equipment most often used for these microwave systems includes a spectrum analyzer to display signal characteristics and a frequency counter capable of displaying an actual frequency of operation. Power meters measure how much energy is being transmitted or received, and an oscilloscope checks waveform performance. Carrier or waveform generators, voltmeters, field strength or signal level meters (SLMs), and volt-ohmmeters may also be used to test a microwave system.

Microwave channels in the 13- and 18-GHz bands commonly used by CATV operators must be licensed by the FCC.

4.2 TVRO EQUIPMENT

Satellite receiving equipment, if required, is housed at the headend. If the headend can receive, but not send, video transmissions, the site is known as a *television receive only* (TVRO) site. Most video transmissions by satellite have been at C band (4-GHz down-link frequency and 6-GHz up-link frequency), but Ku band (12-GHz down-link and 14-GHz up-link) is expected to become increasingly popular for private satellite networks. (See Fig. 4.5.) Basically, the elements of a complete satellite receiving station include the parabolic reflector, a low noise amplifier, a frequency down-converter, and a receiver.

Antennas (a reflector plus signal feed) are designed to concentrate weak RF signals received from a satellite and redirect them to a focal point off the surface of the reflector. (See Fig. 4.6.) At the focal point, a feedhorn collects the energy and passes it to a *low-noise amplifier* (LNA). A single-feed antenna collects signals from one satellite at a time. A multiple-feed antenna collects signals from two or more satellites located close together in the satellite arc. The multibeam feed uses two or more feedhorns to collect signals from more than one focal point.

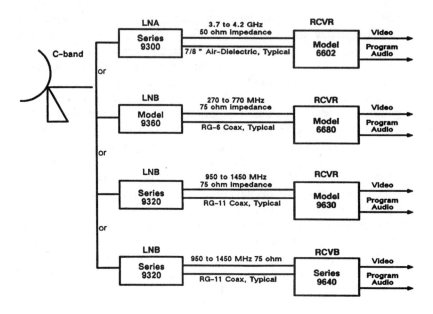

Figure 4.5 Several satellite transmission paths. (Courtesy of Scientific-Atlanta.)

Figure 4.6 Reflector antenna. (Courtesy of Scientific-Atlanta.)

A prime-focus feed antenna reflects signals off the reflector surface to a point where a feedhorn and LNA are located. Sometimes a *low-noise converter* (LNC) or *low-noise block converter* (LNB) are used instead. The LNA is the first active device in the receiving system and amplifies received signals about 50 dB. The LNB additionally down-converts the received frequencies to about 450 to 1500 MHz. The LNC typically down-converts the received signal to the standard 70-MHz IF accepted by most commercial satellite receivers.

A Cassegrain antenna actually reflects a signal twice. Signals are first reflected toward a subreflector at the focal point. From there the signals are reflected toward a feedhorn positioned at the center surface of the reflector. Some antennas use an offset feed system that concentrates received signals to the lip of the antenna.

Antenna gain is a function of several factors. In general, the larger is the reflector, the higher is the gain. Antenna gain is proportional to the square root of the frequency: a doubling of frequency received boosts gain four times. Any imperfections in the surface of the reflector (mechanical damage such as a dent or manufacturing irregularities) will decrease gain. A typical antenna is about 60% efficient.

The receiver contains processing circuits, including a frequency converter (unless an LNC is used on the antenna), bandpass filter and amplifier, discriminator and video processor, and audio processor. (See Fig. 4.7.) The single down-converter takes the original 4-GHz signal and changes it in one step to the 70-MHz IF. Dual down-converters make the signal conversion in two steps, 810 MHz in the first step and 70 MHz in the second step, thus avoiding some of the filtering normally required when the single down-conversion process is used. If an LNB was used on the antenna, a similar block conversion circuit in the receiver again down-converts to the 70-MHz IF. The discriminator and video processor detect the presence of a video signal and filter it to a 4.2-MHz bandwidth. The audio processor finds, filters, and demodulates the audio subcarrier information in the signal.

4.3 OFF-AIR RECEPTION

Antennas and signal processors are responsible for receiving off-air TV signals and preparing them for transportation on a coaxial cable network. (See Fig. 4.8.) Two types of antennas are usually used for off-air TV signal reception: the Yagi antenna and the log periodic antenna. The Yagi is a single-frequency antenna tuned for a specific channel. The log

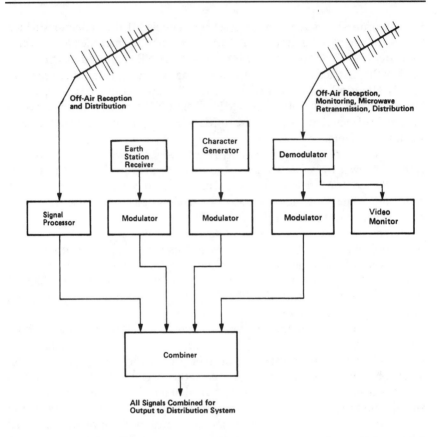

Figure 4.7 Broadband headend components. (Courtesy of Scientific-Atlanta.)

periodic antenna can receive a wider range of frequencies. A single log periodic antenna might be tuned for the low band, high band, and ultra high frequency (UHF) band, for example. These antennas, however, can be designed to receive a single channel or two adjacent channels.

Received signals from either antenna are fed into a signal processor, of which there are several types. The demodulator processor takes the off-air signal, strips away the RF carrier, and adjusts signal levels before reprocessing the baseband, or original, video and audio signals with a new RF carrier for transportation on the cable network. Sometimes called a *mod-demod,* or *demod processor,* it is the most complex form of signal processor. (See Fig. 4.9.)

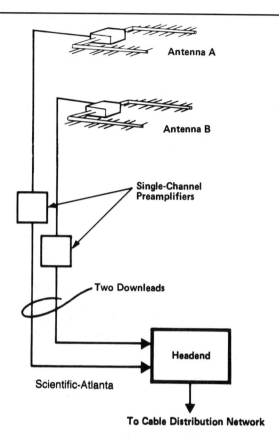

Figure 4.8 Off-air antennas. (Courtesy of Scientific-Atlanta.)

The heterodyne processor mixes the incoming off-air signals with those produced by an internal oscillator to produce a third frequency. This lower frequency signal is then adjusted and up-converted to the desired frequency for network use. This signal processing method is currently one of the most common in the CATV industry.

A simpler, older, and, in many ways, less effective device is the strip amplifier processor. It basically consists of a separate RF amplifier for each channel that is carried on the network. Sometimes called a *strip amplifier* or *straight-through processor,* the strip amp simply amplifies a received signal on its original frequency. Early strip amps did not reject unwanted signals very well and provided only marginal control of the aural and video carrier levels. AGC was also limited. Present-day strip amplifiers should provide better AGC.

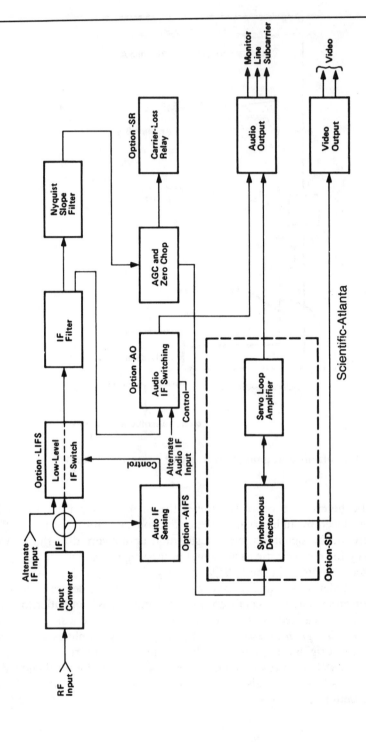

Figure 4.9 Television demodulator. (Courtesy of Scientific-Atlanta.)

Sometimes the received off-air signal is at a very low level, causing carrier-to-noise problems at the signal processor input. Under such conditions a preamplifier is often used to boost the signal level. A preamplifier operates on very much the same principle as an LNA on a satellite receiving antenna. It is designed to quickly amplify a very weak signal prior to its processing. The important thing in preamplifiers is low response to any frequencies other than the single frequency of interest. Also helpful is the placement of a bandpass filter just ahead of the preamplifier.

Pilot carriers are required for amplifiers that do not have the ability to read a modulated carrier (an RF signal mixed with baseband information). If required, those pilot carriers are inserted at the headend by crystal-controlled carrier generators.

The various RF frequencies used on a broadband network must be combined before they leave the headend, and this function is accomplished by a *combiner*. In essence, a combiner acts like a series of directional couplers. As with signals traveling toward the headend from all other outlying points on the network, a directional coupler which splits signals in one direction will combine signals coming from the reverse direction. (See Fig. 4.10.)

Alternating current power supplies often are installed in headends to power distribution cables downstream. A power inserter that passes ac is used to couple the supply to the outbound signal path.

Also found on the outbound signal path are filters to separate high frequencies on the outbound path and low frequencies on the return path.

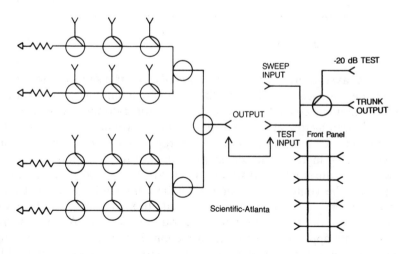

Figure 4.10 Combining network block diagram.

4.4 COAXIAL CABLE

In a sense, coaxial cable (see Fig. 4.11) is the heart of the distribution system. Virtually all other components are designed to put signals on the cable, to take them off, or to compensate for the energy-absorbing characteristics of the cable itself. Part of the actual design of a coaxial cable comes about because of the frequencies of energy actually carried by the cable itself. At low frequencies it is a relatively simple matter to conduct electrical energy. At radio frequencies, on the other hand, any piece of wire longer than about one tenth of a wavelength will act as an antenna (both receiving and radiating signals). When electrical current passes through a single conductor, an electrical field is created that radiates out from the conductor, and a magnetic field surrounds the conductor. Acting in unison, the two forces tend to create signal emissions. One method for nullifying these forces is to use two conductors in parallel with the current flowing in opposite directions. Then the currents at any point would produce fields that are equal and opposite, and the emissions will cancel each other. Such a transmission line is said to be *balanced.*

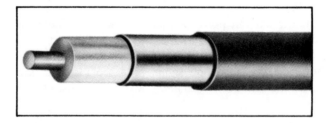

Figure 4.11 Coaxial cable.

A coaxial cable, however, is an *unbalanced* transmission line. It situates one conductor inside the other, with both sharing a common axis (hence the name *coaxial*). The center conductor transmits the signals, and the outer conductor, also called the *sheath,* is grounded. Grounding the outer conductor tends to contain the energy on the center conductor and prevent signal ingress. The coaxial placement of the two conductors does, however, create a situation where the electrical and magnetic fields generated by the center conductor cannot be completely canceled by the current in the outer conductor. So, in addition, one or more layers of shielding material typically surround the outer conductor. An outer jacket is commonly applied for abrasion protection. For cables that will be submersed under water a flooding compound surrounds the conductors; cables that will be directly buried in the ground can take a tough outer covering called *armor.*

Larger trunk and distribution cables usually have a solid aluminum sheath, whereas direct-burial cables may have a corrugated copper sheath. The center conductor can be made of solid copper or copper-clad aluminum. Drop cables sometimes have a copper-clad steel center conductor. Copper-clad aluminum works just as well as solid copper as a conductor, although both steel and aluminum have much higher electrical resistance than copper. Unlike power signals, which will travel through the full cross section of a conductor, RF energy travels only on the outer surface of a conductor. This phenomenon, known as *skin effect,* means that a copper-clad conductor will offer only slightly less resistance to signal flow than solid copper will.

The center conductor is held in place by a foam dielectric material or by spaced plastic disks if the cable uses an air dielectric. In addition to acting as a spacing material, the dielectric also functions as an insulator in foamed cables. Modern dielectric foam is basically a plastic into which millions of tiny air or gas bubbles have been injected. Cables designed for underground use, however, may use a solid, or nonfoamed, polyethylene dielectric. Large trunk cables are made with a foamed polystyrene (Styrofoam). These Styrofoam dielectric cables and air dielectric cables are generally referred to as *low-loss cables* because of their superior attenuation properties.

Maintaining the centering of both cables on the same axis is quite important. The relationship between the two conductors in space, not physical size, but the ratio of the diameters of the center and outer conductors determines the characteristic impedance, or electrical resistance, of the cable. Specifically, it is the relationship between the outer diameter of the center conductor, the inner diameter of the outer conductor, and the dielectric constant that determines characteristic impedance. Thus it is possible to make cables of diameters from 1 in to 0.412 in that all have the same characteristic impedance of 75 Ω. When the ratio between the two conductors is changed, either through manufacturing irregularity or physical damage (a kink or dent), there is a loss of characteristic impedance. That loss causes undesirable signal reflections. The exhortations of cable manufacturers to be careful when handling coaxial cable are well founded.

On the other hand, whereas the ratio of the conductors can change without altering the impedance, the physical size of the conductors and the qualities of the dielectric material do affect attenuation. (See Fig. 4.12.) Larger-center conductors do not lose as much signal as do smaller-center conductors. That is why 1-in or 0.750-in cable, rather than smaller-diameter cables, are used for transporting signals long distances. Drop cable, with the smallest physical diameter, causes the greatest amount of signal attenuation. Thus, it is used only for the last 100 ft of signal transportation to link the network and a user port.

ATTENUATION = FUNCTION OF DIAMETER

	dB/100 ' @ 450 MHz	FT/20dB
RG-59U	7.00	286'
.412∅	2.05	976'
.750∅	1.15	1739'
1.125∅	.75	2667'

$$\frac{1.125\varnothing}{RG\text{-}59} = 9.3$$

∅ = Diameter

Figure 4.12 Attenuation is a function of diameter.

At 450 MHz, for example, a typical RG-59 drop cable will lose about 7 dB in 100 ft. A piece of 0.412-in cable at the same frequency will lose only 2.05 dB over 100 ft. A 100-ft piece of 0.750-in cable will lose 1.15 dB at 450 MHz, but a 100-ft section of 1.125-in cable will lose only 0.75 dB. This has implications for system design, especially amplifier placement. A section of 0.412-in cable will generally require an amplifier every 976 ft. A section of 0.750-in cable will need an amplifier about every 1739 ft. A section of 1.125-in cable will need an amplifier only after running 2667 ft.

For cable hanging exposed outdoors, where summer temperatures can rise to 100° and winter temperatures can go as low as 0°, there can be as much as 2-dB change in attenuation over a single cable span (between any two amplifiers) over the course of a year. An equivalent 2 dB of change would be added for every additional cable span and amplifier in cascade. In this regard, lowered attenuation causes as many problems as increased attenuation. On a very cold day, for example, as attenuation decreases, signal levels will rise. That can overload the amplifiers and increase signal distortion if automatic temperature compensation is not provided. Generally speaking, buried cable will not be subjected to noticeable temperature variation. Likewise, cable in hospital settings will not be subject to much temperature variation over a year's time. Under such relatively benign conditions, AGC and ASC really are optional.

The type of dielectric used makes a difference, as does the density of the foam dielectric used. Air has a dielectric constant of about 1.0, foamed polyethylene about 1.5, and solid polyethylene about 2.3. The lower the dielectric constant is, the lower the attenuation will be.

It is also important to know the attenuation properties of coaxial cable and how attenuation varies with frequency, distance, cable size, dielectric, and temperature. As a general rule, cable attenuation varies about 1% for each 10° of temperature change, increasing with higher temperatures and decreasing with lower temperatures.

Cable attenuation is frequency dependent. (See Fig. 4.13.) Roughly, attenuation doubles as frequency quadruples. At 55 MHz (channel 2) attenuation is half that at 210 MHz (channel 13). In general, amplifier spacing and gain levels assume that normal ambient operating temperature is 68°F and that attenuation is assumed to be at the highest frequency carried by the system.

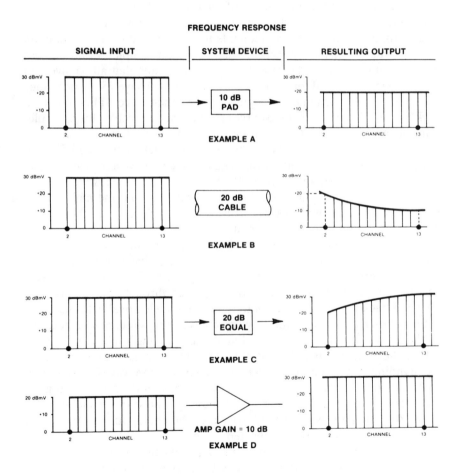

Figure 4.13 Attenuation is frequency dependent. (Courtesy of Texscan.)

Cable attenuation varies with distance: the greater the length of cable, the greater the attenuation, and, as noted before, the smaller the cable diameter, the greater the attenuation.

Temperature can cause cable expansion or contraction. All materials in a coaxial cable have a *coefficient of expansion*. This coefficient is simply a measure of a material's tendency to expand per degree of temperature change. A 2000-foot span of cable experiencing a 50° F temperature swing will contract about 1.33 ft in length from high temperature to low temperature. For this reason, expansion loops are always placed just before a piece of cable enters an active or passive device housing and at all outdoor pole attachments.

We have seen the importance of maintaining the 75-Ω characteristic impedance of a coaxial cable in a broadband communication systems. It is also important to match components to the cable in order to maintain the 75-Ω characteristic impedance. If a tap, splitter, coupler, or fitting does not maintain 75-Ω impedance well (one must assume that all passive and active devices designed for a broadband network will have 75-Ω impedance as a goal), some portion of the signal entering the device will be reflected back toward the transmission source. Nonterminated cable, for example, will reflect virtually 100% of the transmitted energy back toward the transmission site. Physical breaks in the cable or cracks have the effect of changing the impedance and causing signal reflections. When a video signal is being transmitted, the visible effect on receivers is *ghosting*, a faint version of the signal slightly displaced horizontally from the main signal. Such impedance mismatches can cause bit error rates to increase if the strength of the reflection is too great.

Such reflections cause waves that appear to stand along the line, called *voltage standing waves*. The transmitted, or incident wave, strikes a device inserted into the cable or some irregularity within the cable itself. Part of the energy is fully absorbed and passed through, but a portion is reflected back toward the transmitter. Where the electrical fields have the same polarity (positive in the forward and reverse directions or negative in the forward and reverse directions), the standing wave is increased. Where the electrical fields have different polarities (negative and positive), the standing waves tend to cancel. Although the sine waves are continuously moving, the zero cross points are coincident, or the same. That gives the appearance of a wave that is not moving, hence the name *standing wave*. A standing wave is a combination of the energy in the original, or incident, wave as well as the reflected wave.

A method of measuring the degree of mismatch is the *voltage standing wave ratio* (VSWR), the ratio between the maximum and minimum voltages on the line. A perfect transmission line would have a VSWR of 1:1.

A lower limit of about 1.5:1 should be maintained at all times, and a desirable standard is 1.1:1. The amount of reflected signal is called *return loss* when it applies to passives or actives inserted into the cable. (See Fig. 4.14.) When the reflected signal is caused by discontinuities in the cable itself, the term *structural return loss* is used. When devices such as taps are specified for return loss performance, the number cited means that reflections will be sent back a certain number of decibels below the level of the incident carrier. A 20-dB tap, for example, reflects signals back toward the source 20 dB below the level of the incident signal. Typical return loss figures for various devices are 16 dB for amplifiers, 20 to 22 dB for taps, and 30 dB for coaxial cable and connectors. Return loss, then, is a measurement of the magnitude of the standing wave created by a device attached to a coaxial cable.

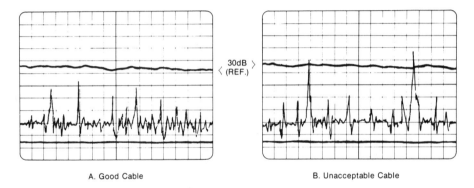

A. Good Cable   B. Unacceptable Cable

Figure 4.14 Typical scope traces for good and bad cable (return loss test). (Courtesy of *CED*.)

If some type of discontinuity appears at a regular interval in a piece of coaxial cable (possibly by the manufacturing process or equal spacing of tap or amplifier points), a phenomenon known as *periodicity* can arise. Periodicity is the tendency for reflections caused by devices or cable imperfections at regular intervals to add because they are in phase. Given enough repetitions of the in-phase reflections, signal power at a single frequency and all the harmonics of that frequency will be reduced. A typical method for avoiding periodicity is to place amplifiers and taps at random rather than at regular distances from each other.

Coaxial cable offers resistance to RF signals passing through it, and it attenuates power signals: the longer the cable, the greater the resistance, and the larger the center conductor, the smaller the resistance. Called *dc loop resistance*, or simply loop resistance, it is an important variable to consider when you decide where to place ac power supplies. The basic design principle is to place the last amplifier served by a single supply in a location where the minimum voltage required to operate that amplifier can be delivered by the supply after loop losses are deducted.

4.5 DIRECTIONAL COUPLERS

A *directional coupler* is used to divide or combine signals flowing through trunk and feeder cables when an unequal signal flow is desired. (See Fig. 4.15.) Directional couplers are often used in amplifiers to tap off small amounts of energy for feeding bridger amplifiers, test points, and AGC or ASC circuits. The output legs of a directional coupler are designed to produce an unequal output level, whereas a *splitter* is used to divide or combine signals equally.

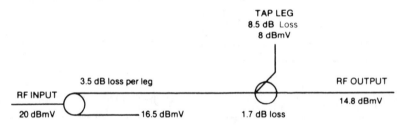

(a) *Typical Signal Levels*

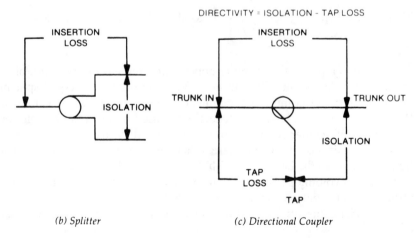

(b) *Splitter*   (c) *Directional Coupler*

Directional Aspects in Cable Systems

Figure 4.15 Passive devices. (Courtesy of *CED*.)

The important parameters for a directional coupler are insertion loss, tap loss, isolation, and directivity. *Insertion loss* is the amount of power lost from input to output of the through leg of the tap. Insertion losses for directional couplers are usually low: 1.5 dB for an 8-dB tap, 1.2 dB for a 12-dB tap, and 0.8 dB for a 16-dB tap. *Tap loss* refers to the amount of power diverted from the through leg to the tap port. *Isolation* refers to the degree to which reflections or spurious products are kept from the tap port and the through leg output port. Good isolation means high loss at the through leg output port to any signals going to the tap port. The higher the isolation is between the tap port and the through leg output port, the better is the device. A coupler with 8 dB of tap loss might have 25 dB of isolation. A coupler with 16 dB of tap loss might have 40 dB of isolation. *Directivity* refers to the ratio of power output at the tap port of the coupler when the signal is fed through the input side of the coupler compared to the power output of the tap port when the signal is fed through the output port of the coupler. Directivity can also be described as the difference between tap loss and isolation loss. Basically, directivity is a measure of coupler efficiency.

Splitters also are power dividers but are designed to divide input power evenly between two output ports. The characteristic impedance remains 75 Ω but the power is reduced by 3 dB on each of the two output ports. (See Fig. 4.16.) Three-way and four-way splitters are nothing more than combinations of two-way splitter circuits. On a three-way splitter one of the split output legs is again divided in two, adding another 3 dB of loss and producing output legs that are 6 dB lower than the original input signal. The result is one output port at 3 dB below input level and two ports at 6 dB below input level. A four-way splitter is a combination of three power-dividing circuits that produces four outputs, each of which is reduced in power 6 dB from the input power level. An eight-way splitter simply repeats the process once more for each of the four output ports to produce signal levels at each of the eight ports that is roughly 10 dB per leg lower than the original input signal.

The typical insertion loss (power removed from input to output ports) of a two-way splitter is about 3.5 to 4 dB per leg. Recall that 3 dB represents a signal level drop of 50% and that some additional loss above the theoretical 3 dB is caused by tap inefficiency. If input were 10 dB, output would be about 6 to 6.5 dB on each leg. A three-way splitter will have an insertion loss of about 7 dB on two legs and a loss of 3.5 dB or so on a single leg. A four-way splitter would have about 3 dB output on all four output legs.

Taps are passive devices designed to tap signal energy off a cable to feed a drop cable. Taps generally are available in two-port, four-port, and eight-port versions. Known as *multitaps* (see Fig. 4.17), each of these devices basically is a combination of a directional coupler and one or more

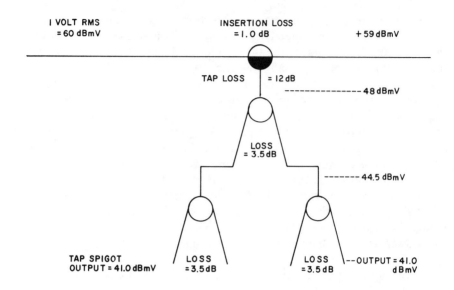

Figure 4.16 Multitap losses. (Courtesy of Magnavox CATV.)

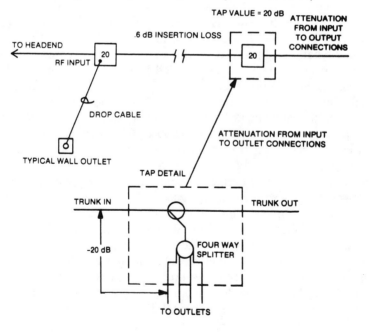

Figure 4.17 The multitap. (Courtesy of *CED*.)

splitter sections arranged to produce a given output value. A 12-dB directional coupler followed by a four-way splitter would produce a four-port tap with signal levels reduced 19 dB from input. The losses come from the combined effect of 12-dB tap loss and two 3.5-dB splitter sections. Actual loss varies from theoretical because of the inefficiency of the splitting circuit itself.

Taps come in numerous values, which refer to the total amount of signal attenuation of the tap. These dB values usually are indicated on the tap itself and can run from the high 30s to 4. (See Fig. 4.18.) A 30-dB tap, for example, removes 30 dB of signal from the line. Insertion loss, as opposed to tap loss, varies with the tap value. Recall that insertion loss refers to the difference in power between the input and output ports of the through leg of the tap. Basically, the higher the value of the tap is, the lower the insertion loss is. A 35-dB tap can have insertion loss as low as 0.4 dB, and an 11-dB tap can have insertion loss of 3.5 dB.

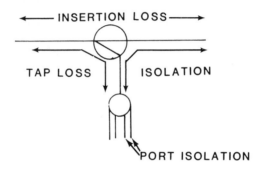

Figure 4.18 Multiport tap. (Courtesy of Wavetek.)

A *power inserter* is a device that resembles a splitter or directional coupler. Its function is to put ac power onto a coaxial cable without disturbing the RF signals. Filters inside the power inserter allow power to flow onto the cable but not back to the power source itself. The power inserter is used to couple power supplies to the network.

A *terminator* is a specialized connector designed to cap the end of a cable path by fully absorbing all the RF energy and ac power flowing toward it. (See Fig. 4.19.)

Among the more common, and most important, passives found on a broadband network is the *connector*, a device used to join two lengths of cable or a piece of cable to a port. F-type connectors, used on the RG-59 and RG-6 drop cables, are literally used on every device connected to

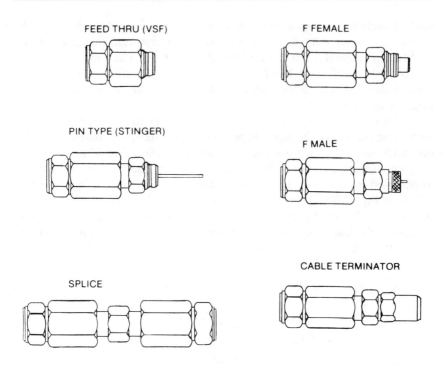

Figure 4.19 Connectors.

a length of drop cable. (See Fig. 4.20.) Although it is not an expensive item, the F-connector and the drop cable probably account for 75 to 80% of the operational problems encountered by many CATV system operators. The problem has several facets but generally revolves around improper connectorization: the method used to prepare the cable for attachment of the connector and the method used to crimp the connector onto the drop cable. Electrical problems that result from improper connectorization include signal attenuation, signal leakage or ingress, or moisture ingress. If there is a weak link in a broadband network, look for it at the drop-cable-to-device interface.

4.6 AMPLIFIERS

An *amplifier* is an electronic device that takes weak, low-amplitude input signal and reproduces it as a higher-amplitude output. Amplifiers are used in broadband networks to compensate for signal losses introduced by coaxial cable. Amplifiers can be classified by purpose as trunk, bridger,

Figure 4.20 F-connector.

distribution, and LEs. Trunk amplifiers are designed for the backbone cable network and accept a low input level (possibly 10 to 12 dBmV) and reproduce the signal at higher amplitude (possibly 20 to 28 dB of gain) with minimum distortion, since it is intended that trunk signals might need to run some distance. Output from a trunk amplifier can run anywhere from 32 to 34 dBmV. Trunk amplifiers will typically be spaced about 20 dB apart, this being the length of cable required to attenuate signals at the highest frequency by 20 dB.

A bridger amplifiers is used to tap RF energy off a trunk cable and supply it to a feeder network. It runs at high gain, commonly 47 to 51 dBmV, because it is not intended to feed more than two or three additional amplifiers in its cascade. A bridger circuit is often located in the same housing as a trunk station. Because of its higher gain, the bridger amplifier causes more distortion than a trunk amplifier does. A bridger amplifier often will feed as many as four separate feeder cables. When one cable is fed, the insertion loss is 0.0 dBmV. When two cables are fed, the insertion loss is 3.5 dBmV. When three cables are fed, the insertion loss is 3.5 dBmV on one leg and 6.5 dBmV on the other two legs. A four-cable feed has insertion loss of 6.5 dBmV on each leg.

LEs are used after bridger amplifiers to deliver a signal to user ports on the feeder network. They are smaller, less expensive, less power-hungry devices than trunk amplifiers. They take higher input signals, have less stringent performance specifications, and introduce more noise and distortion than trunk amplifiers do.

A newer type of amplifier recently developed for the CATV industry is the *distribution amplifier,* which basically puts a trunk amplifier circuit into a housing the size of the LE, omitting some of the "bells and whistles" but preserving the basic advantages of the trunk amplification circuits. The advantage is that the distribution amplifier, although less expensive than a trunk amplifier, does not present the same cascade limitations as the standard LE. Scientific-Atlanta's distribution amplifier for example, is designed to be modular. It can be configured as a conventional trunk station with AGC circuits, as a standard LE, or as a bridger amplifier. This multipurpose amplifier also contains internal splitters and couplers to make installation easier. A distribution amplifier might cost half as much as a conventional LE. Its advantage over a trunk station, in LANs or low-density CATV applications, is that it runs at higher levels than conventional trunk amplifiers so fewer amplifier stations are needed to cover any distance and feeder cable lengths are reduced.

Amplifiers can also be classified by the type of circuits used in the station itself. Currently available amplifiers use push-pull, parallel hybrid (sometimes called power-doubling), feedforward, or quad technology using two tandem parallel hybrid circuits. Which type of technology is best depends on the situation. For example, the length of cable runs and how the number of ports are planned, will influence the choice of technology in some instances. Small networks may only need rack-mounted amplifiers in the headend. As network size grows, so will the demands for mainstations, bridgers, distribution amplifiers, or LEs.

Push-pull is a two-stage amplification technique used by all current amplifier manufacturers to improve distortion performance, especially second-order artifacts. (See Fig. 4.21.) Second-order is a harmonic at double the frequency of the original signal. It was not a problem when amplifiers only had to pass the very high frequency (VHF) bands. But second-order products produced by a single gain-stage amplifier produced heavy second-order products in the midband (108 to 174 MHz). So as broadband systems expanded beyond the 54- to 108-MHz and 174- to 216-MHz ranges, single-ended (single gain-stage) amplifier circuits were replaced by push-pull circuits.

Push-pull uses a form of phase reversal to achieve second-order canceling effects. Each gain stage has a power splitter and an inverter, two gain circuits, and then a power combiner and an inverter. The purpose of

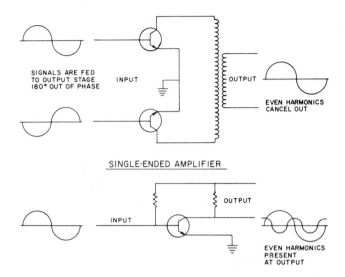

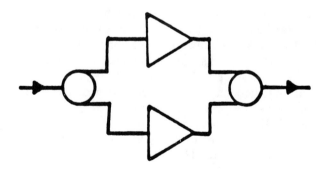

Figure 4.21 Push-pull amplifier. (Courtesy of Magnavox CATV.)

this configuration is to cancel the even harmonics by putting them 180° out of phase with each other. When the harmonics recombined, they tend to cancel.

Power-doubling or *parallel hybrid* technology is used to improve distortion performance while boosting output. (See Fig. 4.22.) The technique uses two sets of push-pull gain circuits at each gain stage and provides an additional 3 dB of gain over conventional push-pull circuits.

Figure 4.22 Parallel hybrid circuit.

Quadrapower is simply a parallel arrangement of two power-doubling circuits, again with the intention of improving distortion performance by about 2.5 to 3 dB. (See Fig. 4.23.) Quadrapower amplifiers run pretty hot but draw less current than feedforward amplifiers. Typically, quadrapower technology is used for very large urban CATV networks.

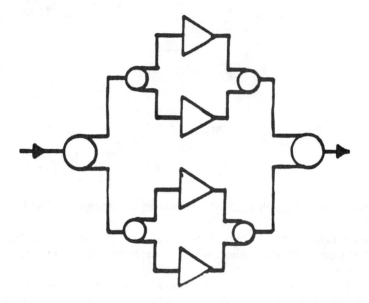

Figure 4.23 Quadrapower.

Feedforward uses cancellation effects to improve distortion performance for very long cascades. A feedforward circuit consists of two amplifier hybrids (a main amplifier and an error amplifier) and two delay line circuits. (See Fig. 4.24.) The circuit amplifies the distortion signals twice but inverts the phase 180°. When they are remixed, the signals cancel, leaving the amplified main signal. Feedforward is very useful for large MANs but less useful for a broadband LAN.

Should feedforward technology be used? Generally, no. It is a rare network that has amplifier cascades long enough to justify the cost or capabilities of feedforward. How about power-doubling? Usually it will not add more noise, but it will add more distortion. However, it does offer a form of redundancy. On the other hand, LANs typically are not distortion-limited. Most broadband LANs are relatively lightly loaded compared with the typical CATV network. Consequently, intermodulation products are reduced.

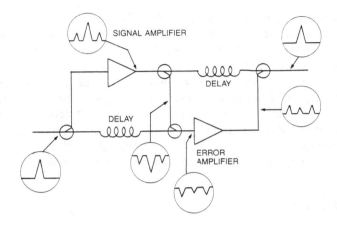

ADVANTAGE:

    20 dB DISTORTION IMPROVEMENT
    IMPROVED RELIABILITY

COMPROMISE:

    COMPLEXITY
    HIGHER CURRENT

Figure 4.24 Feedforward amplifiers. (Courtesy of General Instrument Corporation.)

Amplifier choices also are affected by the bandwidth used by a given broadband LAN and the array of monitoring features desired. If status monitoring or power supply or amplifier module redundancy is desired, only certain models made by certain manufacturers will do. Some amplifiers can be fitted with AGC and ASC. Others can only be adjusted manually.

As a general rule of thumb, trunk amplifiers (main stations) incorporating bridger circuits are used when networks have cable runs of a mile or more. Bridger amplifiers are used to tap signals off a trunk amplifier for distribution to a feeder leg. These amplifiers are commonly located inside main-station housings and sometimes are found at any point on the trunk where a feeder leg is needed. They can also be used near the end of a trunk line in place of a trunk amplifier. Bridgers are operated at high gain (48 or 50 dB) and are typically followed by a maximum of two LEs in cascade. Large campus-sized networks will use trunk, bridger, distribution, or LEs in combination.

On smaller networks it is often possible to use distribution amplifiers or very high gain LE amplifiers, which cost less. A tapped-trunk design, for example, is often a solution for a relatively small network and uses LEs or distribution amps exclusively. This low-cost solution has workstation ports tapped directly off the main trunk. Still smaller networks may not need line amplification at all and can use rack-mounted devices. (See Fig. 4.25.)

TAPPED TRUNK

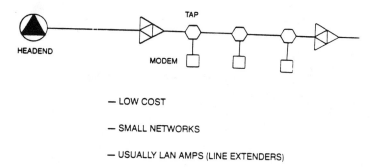

— LOW COST

— SMALL NETWORKS

— USUALLY LAN AMPS (LINE EXTENDERS)

LAN MAINSTATIONS AND LAN AMPS

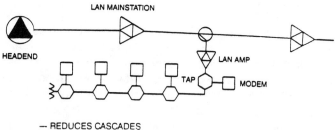

— REDUCES CASCADES

— REDUCES FREQUENCY RESPONSE PROBLEMS WITH PASSIVES

— SIMPLIFIES PATH LOSS CALCULATION

Figure 4.25 LAN architectures. (Courtesy of General Instrument Corporation.)

Moderately large single-cable networks (a factory network with risers, or example) will require a more traditional design using trunks and feeders to reduce main-station cascades and optimize frequency response by reducing the total number of passives on the trunkline. Such a network can often be constructed by using amplifiers such as the Jerrold SJ series for the trunkline and JLEs or IDA-450s for feeder legs.

Large campus- or metropolitan-sized single-cable networks require standard trunk, bridger, and feeder designs usually found on CATV networks and will use standard mainstations like the C-COR LAN-5000 and LAN-6000 series and LEs like the LAN-100 and LAN-101 series. (See Fig. 4.26.) The 5000 series amplifiers run 5 to 112 MHz in the return path and 150 to 450 MHz forward. Pair it with the LAN-100. The 6000 series runs 5 to 186 MHz in the reverse path and 222 to 450 MHz in the forward path. Pair it with the LAN-101.

General Instrument's Jerrold Division makes the X-2000 series mainstation in midsplit and high-split versions. It also makes the SJ series midsplit main station, a most cost-effective device or some networks. (See Fig. 4.27.) The JLE series distribution amplifiers are high-gain devices (30 or 37 dB forward, 30 return) used in LE applications with Jerrold's main stations.

For subsplit systems, the Magnavox 440-MHz and 330-MHz main stations and companion MLE series LEs are another option. The midsplit trunk amplifiers made by Magnavox come in 450- and 330-MHz versions.

Likewise, the Texscan Series 1000 or Series 2000 main stations can be paired with Texscan's Series 3000 LEs for feeder legs. The 2000 models take bridger modules; the 1000 models do not. The frequency split for both trunk amplifiers is 150 to 450 MHz forward and 55 to 120 MHz return.

A new option is to use Scientific-Atlanta's 6501 or 6502 distribution amplifier. This versatile model can be configured as either a trunk station or LE and is clearly the model Scientific-Atlanta sells most often for LAN applications. The company also makes high-split and midsplit 450-MHz main stations as well as LEs in 330-, 400-, 450-, and 550-MHz versions.

The Scientific-Atlanta, General Instrument, Magnavox, and Texscan amplifiers are normally manufactured at 450 or 550 MHz.

Catel Telecommunications makes a 440-MHz model MX main station with 174- to 440-MHz bandwidth in the forward path and 5 to 108 MHz in the return path. Gain range is 10 dB, however, in contrast to the more typical 13- to 22-dB forward gain and 37-dB reverse gain for main stations.

Augat Broadband has several rack-mounted amplifiers in its product line that are ideal for small broadband networks without need or distribution system amplification. The VFA-450 has forward bandwidth of 450 MHz and gains from 20 to 50 dB. Its companion VRA-200 provides 20 to 40 dB of gain for the return path over the 5- to 200-MHz range. A new

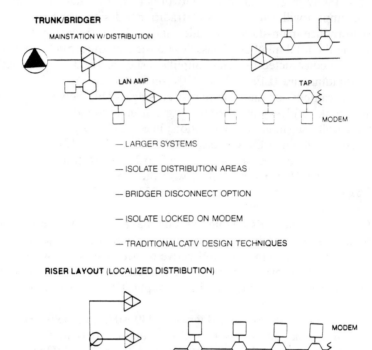

TRUNK/BRIDGER

MAINSTATION W/DISTRIBUTION

LAN AMP

TAP

MODEM

— LARGER SYSTEMS

— ISOLATE DISTRIBUTION AREAS

— BRIDGER DISCONNECT OPTION

— ISOLATE LOCKED ON MODEM

— TRADITIONAL CATV DESIGN TECHNIQUES

RISER LAYOUT (LOCALIZED DISTRIBUTION)

MODEM

TAP

LAN AMP
or
DISTRIBUTION
AMP

— CONVENIENT ACCESS TO AMPLIFIERS

— TIE-IN TO LARGER SYSTEMS

Figure 4.26 LAN architectures. (Courtesy of General Instrument Corporation.)

VFA-550 rack-mounted amplifier runs from 40 to 550 MHz and is available in either a standard hybrid version with gains of 24, 30, and 37 dB or a power-doubling version available in 30- and 34-dB gains. (See Fig. 4.28.)

The company also manufactures the dc-powered Data-450 trunk amplifier with forward passband of 40 to 450 MHz and the companion Data-200 for the reverse path (also dc-powered). The Data-200 has a bandwidth

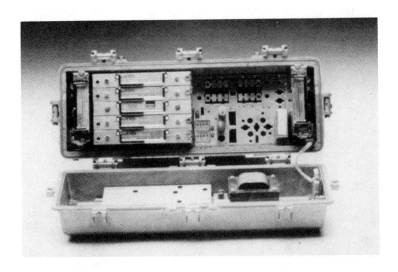

Figure 4.27 X-2000 mainstation.

of 5 to 200 MHz. The BDA amplifier, available in push-pull or power-doubling versions, is designed for midsplit operation indoors. It runs 150 to 450 MHz forward and 5 to 112 MHz reverse.

When a network is expanded, the NE-4 LAN network expander can be quite useful. It allows expansion of a one-port site to a four-port site without system realignment or additional power drain. It is a "no gain, no loss" device with its own power supply. The BLX-2 LE comes in 26- to 44-dB gains in the forward path and 16-dB, 20-dB, or 30-dB gain in the return path. Both 330- and 450-MHz versions are available.

Some leading amplifier manufacturers also have developed dual-cable versions of their main stations and LEs that operate over the passband from MHz 40 or 42 to 450 MHz typically used for dual-cable networks. C-COR Electronics makes the LAN-3000 series outbound trunk amplifier and companion LAN-4000 inbound trunk amplifier. Both operate in the 42- to 450-MHz bands. The LAN-2100 series LE is designed to be run in the traditional two-LE cascade off a trunk line.

General Instrument's Jerrold Division makes versions of its X-2000 series main stations designed for the 40- to 450-MHz passband. The main-station housing is designed to accept two trunk cables. A large network might use the dual-cable X-2000s with SLX-450-1W distribution amplifiers. A smaller network might use the 5.5-lb SLX models as trunk amplifiers. A matching LE is the IDA-450, offering 40 dB of gain. (See Fig. 4.29.)

Specifications

Bandwidth (MHz)	Forward Push-Pull-Hybrid 150-450	Return Push-Pull Hybrid 5-112	Forward Power Doubling Hybrid 150-450
Frequency Response (dB)	±.25	±.25	±.25
Gains Available	30	30, 18	30
Channel Loading	50	18	50
Output Level (dBmV)	45/42	45/42	45/42
Signal-to-Xmod Ratio (dB)	65	76	71
Signal-to-CTB Ratio (dB)	66	78	72
Signal-to-2nd Order Ratio (dB)	71	78	74
Noise Figure (dB)	7	10	7
Gain Range (dB)	6	6	6
Slope Range (dB)	3	6	3
AC Operating Voltage	See Powering Table	See Powering Table	See Powering Table
Return Loss Input and Output	16 dB Typical-14 dB Minimum	16 dB Typical-14 dB Minimum	16 dB Typical-14 dB Minimum

Figure 4.28 Broadband bidirectional data network amplifier. (Courtesy of Augat.)

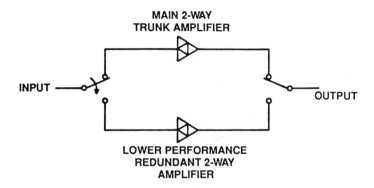

Figure 4.29 Switched active redundancy.

Redundancy is a key design goal for some networks or for some legs of networks, and there are several ways to approach it. One way is to install A/B switches and an alternative signal path at the input and output of each amplifier. If the station fails, the switches can route signals past the station.

Another approach is to use two amplifier modules in the same housing, with a switch to a "cold" backup if the main module fails. (See Fig. 4.30.) The same goal is achieved by collocating a backup amplifier near the primary station. "Hot" standby redundancy could be provided by collocating active and redundant hybrids or modules in the same housing or by running two fully redundant amplifiers side by side. (See Fig. 4.31.)

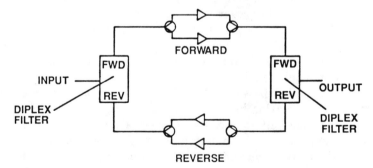

Figure 4.30 Internal redundant FWD/REV trunk amplifier.

C-COR Electronics does offer an active fail-safe amplifier module that is used in the LAN-3000, 4000, 5000, and 6000 trunk stations. Two

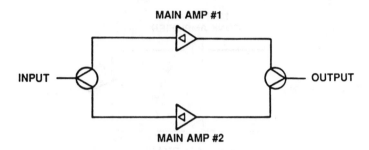

Figure 4.31 External combined amplifiers.

versions are available. A trunk-amplifier-only unit backs up the main forward and reverse paths. The trunk and bridger unit backs up both the
main forward and reverse paths as well as the bridger amplifier. The Quick
Alert status monitoring system is required.

The Jerrold X-2000 main stations are available in redundant configurations that provide backup power packs as well as redundant amplifier
modules. Jerrold's Advanced Status Monitor system is required.

A typical bidirectional trunk amplifier has a two-piece die-cast aluminum housing designed to seal the unit against weather and RF egress
or ingress. (See Fig. 4.32.) A gasket seals the hinged lid to the base.
Convection fins on the housing surface increase the surface area and dis-
sipate heat faster. In addition to the input and output ports for the trunk
cable, there are usually several (as many as four) additional ports for output
to feeder cables. The lid typically is secured with bolts.

Inside the housing, some sort of interconnection chassis is required
to seat the various modules or boards and to provide a signal path for RF
energy in the forward and reverse directions, ac from the cable, and dc
from the power supply to modules in the unit.

High-pass and low-pass filters at its input and output ports are used
to separate signals moving in the forward and reverse paths. (See Fig.
4.33.) Pads and equalizers are used to flatten signal response before it goes
to the actual amplifier circuits in both the forward and return paths.

Basically, the trunk amplifier circuit must do two things. (1) It must
restore the original amplitude of the input signal to the set system operating
level. (2) It also must correct the tilt, or frequency-dependent attenuation,
that coaxial cable imposes. Typically, two gain stages will be used. Each,
for example, might amplify signals 17 dB. Between the two gain stages
there is a slope control that can be manually or automatically adjusted.
The slop control adjusts the signal for flatness (equal amplitude across the
entire passband). Typically, a high-pass filter (see Fig. 4.34) will also be

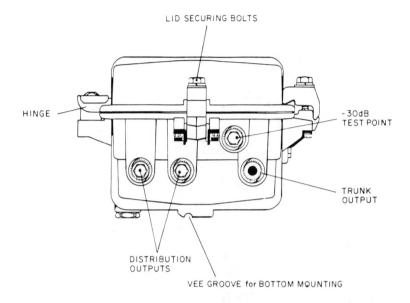

Figure 4.32 5-TH side view (output). (Courtesy of Magnavox CATV.)

used in the forward stage to filter out unwanted signals in the lower frequencies. After filtering, signals will enter the second gain stage before they are directed to the trunk station output and a bridger circuit, if one is used at this station.

Usually signals entering the main station housing first go through an attenuator. Unless signal levels are too high (say, if the cable run immediately preceding the main station were shorter than usual), the attenuator value is zero. Other values are used if the input signal level is too high and must be reduced to the set operating range. Common attenuator values are 0, 3, 6, 9, and 12 dB.

Next, the signal goes through an *equalizer*. (See Fig. 4.35.) The equalizer has the job of producing a flat response across all frequencies of interest. Recall that the higher frequencies will have been attenuated more than the lower frequencies. The equalizer reduces the signals at lower frequencies to match those at the higher passbands. Common equalizer values include 0, 5, 8, 11, 14, 17, and 20 dB.

The first amplification stage is provided by the *preamplifier*, which takes signals from the equalizer and boosts them. Typically, the precise amount of gain specified for this stage is controlled by a gain control circuit that operates manually or automatically (both options are usually available) to control the output and provide a constant signal level. Next, the

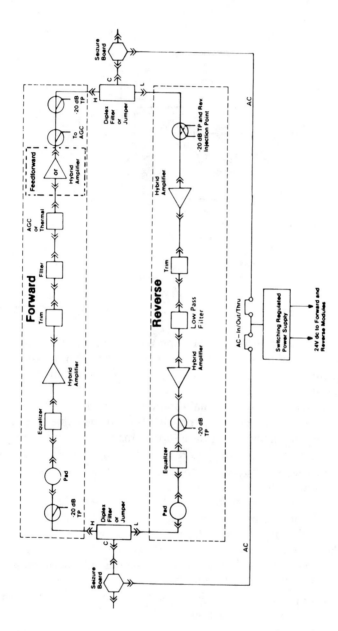

Figure 4.33 Distribution amplifier. (Courtesy of Scientific-Atlanta.)

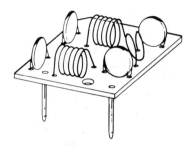

Figure 4.34 High-pass filter board. (Courtesy of Magnavox CATV.)

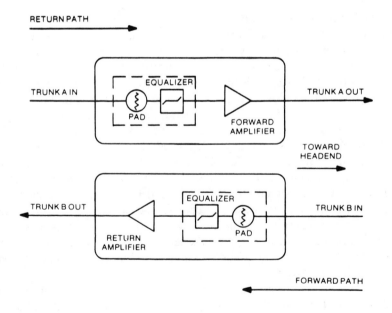

Figure 4.35 Dual cable system amplifier. (Courtesy of *CED*.)

signal passes through a slope control circuit that attenuates the regenerated signal in tapered or tilted fashion: high frequencies are attenuated least, and low frequencies most. The amount of slope should ideally compensate exactly for the equal but opposite tilt to be introduced by the next length of coaxial cable. (See Fig. 4.36.)

To prevent ingress of stray return path signals, a high-pass filter is positioned at the output of the slope control circuit. Forward path signals moving through the amplifier then would enter the second amplification stage. The *postamplifier* contributes a further boost in signal level. If the amplifier station contains a bridger circuit, a directional coupler will tap off part of the signal and feed it to a splitter for distribution to a bridger amplifier circuit and one or more feeder lines.

A typical trunk amplifier might contribute a maximum gain of about 26 dB after internal losses are subtracted. A trunk amplifier also must have an internal power supply that converts ac input voltage into the 24-V dc used to power amplifier modules and circuits. It typically is configured to accept either 30-V ac or 60-V ac input in either quasi-square-wave or square-wave forms.

Bidirectional amplifiers have return path circuits to amplify signals returning to the headend. Typically, return path signals go into a preamplifier stage first, where they might be boosted about 18 dB. Signals out of the preamplifier then enter an attenuator where the signal level is adjusted to the design specification. A slope control circuit might follow. (See Fig. 4.37.) A slope of about 1 dB on a midsplit system would mean that the signal level of the highest return frequency would be 1 dB higher than the signal level at the lowest return frequency.

Communications from any status monitoring transponders located at the amplifier station can be combined with the return path signals just before a low-pass filter is inserted into the signal path. This filter is designed to reject any stray signals from the forward path that may accidentally contaminate the reverse path frequencies. After the signal has passed through the low-pass filter, the second amplification stage boosts signal strength again and feeds the strengthened signals to an attenuator, which sets output levels to design specifications for signal levels into the next amplifier in the cascade.

A typical redundant trunk amplifier will contain the same circuits and maintain the same signal flow as the nonredundant amplifier, but will do so for two fully independent amplification systems in the same housing.

A typical bridger amplifier sends signals only in the forward path. Signals on the return path run through the reverse amplifier. On some amplifiers, there is a slope control circuit located at the input to the bridger circuit that provides 5 or 6 dB of slope control that is manually controlled.

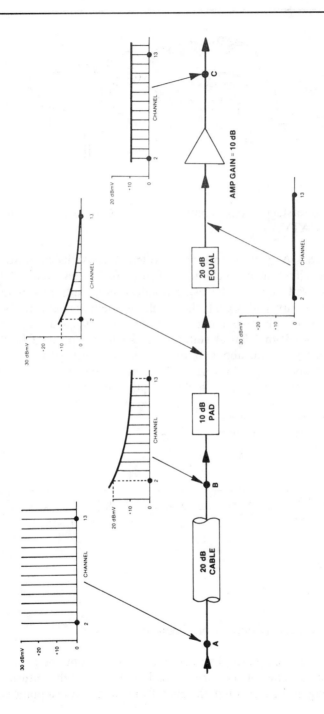

Figure 4.36 System responses. (Courtesy of Texscan.)

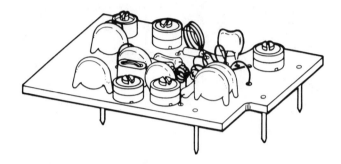

Figure 4.37 Interstage slope control board. (Courtesy of Magnavox CATV.)

(See Fig. 4.38.) A gain control circuit often follows; its purpose is to maintain a specified signal level into the first amplification circuit. A high-pass filter is used between the two amplification circuits to isolate and eliminate any return path signals that might accidentally get into the forward path. Common bridger amplifier gains are 37 to 40 dB, and a common output level is 46 dBmV. Trunk stations are usually set to run at 14 dBmV in the forward path and about 37 dBmV in the return path. Since the typical broadband design does not call for more than two or three LE stations beyond the bridger, the higher output can safely be used.

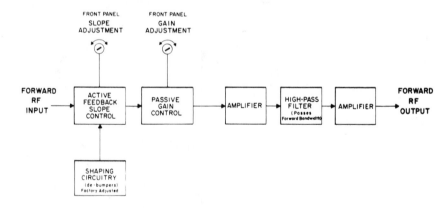

Figure 4.38 Bridger. (Courtesy of Magnavox CATV.)

A typical LE amplifier, like the trunk station, contains two sets of amplifier circuits: one for the forward path and one for the return path. Signals moving in the forward path generally move past a test point before entering a high-pass filter that isolates return path energy. A low-pass filter is used to route ac energy on the cable to the power supply. An attenuator circuit takes signals from the high-pass filter and sets them to the design input level if they are too high. An equalizer circuit flattens the frequency response of the forward signals in case they have tilted while running through the previous length of cable. Typical equalizer values are 0, 3, 6, 9, and 12 dB.

After equalization, the signals are fed into the first gain stage, which might boost signals as much as 16 dB. Gain and slope control stages follow to adjust signal level and frequency response. The second gain stage follows, boosting signals in an amount equal to the first gain stage. Next in the chain is a high-pass filter used to isolate return path signals. After passing by a test point, forward path signals are returned to the feeder cable.

Signals in the return path enter the LE through the output port; the signals are isolated from forward path energy by a low-pass filter before they are fed into a return amplifier module that boosts them by about 24 dB. Slope and gain control circuits follow to adjust signal level and frequency response. Overall output gain might be 19 or 20 dB after internal losses are subtracted. Another low-pass filter is used to isolate forward path signals before the return amplifier's output is coupled to the feeder network again.

Modern broadband amplifiers are reliable devices with MTBF from 12 to 30 years. But some common amplifier problems are caused by technician error rather than by equipment malfunction. If equalizers or pads with the wrong attenuation values are inserted into the amplifier, or if gain and slope controls are not properly adjusted, noise and distortion will occur. If ac power input to the amplifier is low, expect to see hum modulation. Loose screws can cause intermittent signal outages.

When an amplifier does fail mechanically for internal reasons, it is usually a failure of an integrated circuit in one or more stages of the amplifier, a failure of the AGC or ASC circuits, or a failure of the internal power supply. Frequently, the result is a gain in visible noise downstream from the failing amplifier. Older amplifiers using discrete components could suffer transistor, resistor, or capacitor failure. That is not as much a problem with the newer integrated packages.

Unfortunately, all amplifiers introduce some distortion as they boost the amplitude of signals passing through them. The distortions can include noise, amplitude changes, frequency changes, intermodulation, or harmonics.

4.7 POWERING BROADBAND NETWORKS

Amplifiers and other active devices on broadband networks are powered by ac current inserted directly onto the cable itself by power supplies that take commerical power at 117 or 120 V and convert it to 60-V ac. A power inserter, which acts like a directional coupler, is used to couple the power to the network.

When a system is designed, the power supply placement decisions require that the loop resistance of all network cabling be known. Loop resistance, or dc resistance, is a measure of how much voltage is lost as the signal moves through a given cable. Loop resistance typically is specified in ohms per thousand feet of cable. The amount of resistance varies with the size of the cable, type of center conductor, and dielectric. Standard aluminum sheath, solid copper foam dielectric cable of 0.412-in diameter will have loop loss of about 2.03 Ω. Similar cable of 0.5 diameter will have about 1.43 Ω loop resistance, and 0.75 in cable will have roughly 0.62 Ω loop resistance. Cable with copper-clad center conductors will have slightly higher loop resistance, whereas air dielectric cable will have less loop resistance.

The basic design criteria for power supply placement is that the minimum voltage needed to power an active device such as an amplifier must be delivered at all times. If the minimum voltage is 40 V, then 40 V will always be present at that amplifier location. (See Fig. 4.39.) If 44 V is required, then 44 V will always be available at that location. The key parameters, then, are device power draw and loop loss between the devices.

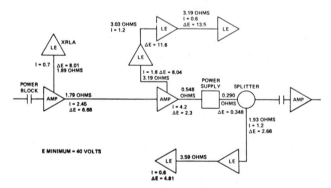

Figure 4.39 60 volt system powering. (Courtesy of *CED*.)

When power supply locations are determined, the first step usually is to prepare a schematic showing all cable placements and amplifier locations required. The amount of loop resistance for the cables and amplifier current draw, taken from manufacturer specifications, is then determined. A calculation of current flow in each cable section, including each active device to be powered, can then be made. The amount of voltage reduction caused by each amplifier and length of cable is then added. Starting at the power insertion point, one can determine voltage levels at the end of each cable section by subtracting all the various voltage reductions from the input value. Each amplifier or other active device should get the minimum voltage required for it to operate. On most broadband networks, however, some form of power protection will be desirable on one or more network legs. This usually is accomplished by the use of standby or *uninterruptible power supplies* (UPS) that have battery backup capabilities. (See Fig. 4.40.)

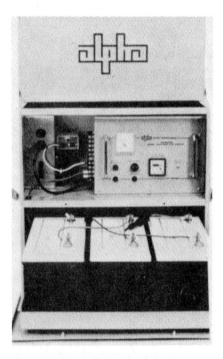

Figure 4.40 Uninterruptible power supply (UPS). (Courtesy of Alpha Industries.)

IBM says that the average computer is subjected to 128.3 power line disturbances each month. That is a pretty good argument for the use of standby or UPS powering. Standby supplies can sense loss of commerical power and will automatically switch to battery power. Typical supplies will run from 2 to 4 h. When commerical power is again available, a charging circuit in the supply will recharge the batteries.

Uninterruptible supplies go a step further and are designed to kick in within a few milliseconds of any sensing of loss of ac power. Actually, there is some confusion about what a "true" UPS is. Some units are designed to run "hot" and are actually on-line all of the time. Such a unit is safely called UPS. On the other hand, some units kick in so quickly (4 ms or so) that they act as *virtual* or *fast transfer* UPS.

A virtual unit provides the same level of protection as "true" UPS but with greater reliability, since the circuits are not cooking constantly. A good ferroresonant UPS will transfer so quickly that a user cannot even see a waveform perturbation on a waveform monitor as the switch occurs. An on-line UPS is more expensive because it must contain redundancy. In essence, it must be overbuilt. Thus, on-line units are heavier and larger, and they run hotter and less efficiently.

UPS units also normally include power-conditioning circuits. Standby units without high-speed transfer switches (which kick on within 4 to 10 ms) might not prevent all loss of data. Uninterruptibles usually work fast enough that no data is lost.

Preventing power outages is important. But outages—complete loss of commerical power—are not usually the cause of most glitches for the PC user. PCs, especially some PC clones, are quite susceptible to dips from 120 to 100 V, for example. In fact, most damage to computer memories is not caused by outages. Voltage fluctuations, transients, and sags are the major culprits. Power conditioning and surge suppression can prevent many of the problems a PC user might encounter. Generally speaking, a PC will not lose data if the switch from ac to dc is made in 4 to 5 ms or less.

Network powering, as opposed to device powering, is a somewhat more complex issue. Many amplifiers, for example, have dc switching supplies that will hold a charge for up to 150 ms—nominally 75 ms. That is long enough for a standby unit to kick in. If cost is an issue, a good Stand By Power Supply (SPS) might do the job for reliable backup powering of a broadband LAN. On the other hand, if data integrity is essential, a UPS, although more expensive, is called for.

Typically, standby units for broadband come in a metal enclosure and contain batteries, chargers, square-wave inverters, and a high-speed switch. Under normal ac powering conditions the inverter is in a state of rest. When ac voltage drops past a predetermined point (15%, for example), the load is switched to the inverter, which draws dc power from the batteries and converts the power to ac.

A UPS is typically on line continuously and maintains output voltage within a percentage of nominal (possibly ±3%, for example). The UPS consists of a rectifier or charger, battery, and inverter and normally converts commerical ac power to dc, which is then used to charge the battery and, in turn, the inverter, which reshapes the dc into ac power.

4.8 MODEMS

All devices connected to a broadband network require the use of an RF modem and network interface software appropriate for the specific protocols being run on the network (802.3 or Ethernet; 802.4 token-passing bus). Devices incorporating both the modem circuitry and the access software are often referred to as *network interface units* (NIUs) or *bus interface units* (BIUs).

The modem converts digital signals produced by the networked device to analog format for transmission on the network. (See Fig. 4.41.) It also converts analog signals coming to the networked device to digital format. Modems have the ability to mix, or modulate, digital information with an appropriate frequency for transmission on the network. The oldest type of RF modem was the fixed-frequency point-to-point modem, designed to link two devices on a permanent basis using a single, dedicated channel. One frequency is set aside for use as a transmitting channel while another different frequency is used as a receiving channel. This method avoids channel conflicts. Traditionally, point-to-point modems have run between 9.6 and 64 kb/s.

Networked modems are more complex. A networked or frequency-agile modem has the ability to vary its transmitting and receiving frequency pairs to take advantage of available channel space or to communicate with more than one device on a network. Modems used on broadband systems traditionally have been asynchronous devices (no internal clocking or continuous synchronization of signal streams between the sending station and the receiving station), although synchronous devices required for interfacing with the IBM computing environment are available. Asynchronous transmission is relatively simple and well suited for lower-speed communications. Synchronous transmission, however, offers much higher speed because the bit streams are commonly clocked by a timing signal embedded in the data or sent along with the data. This allows data to be sent continuously without start or stop bits, thereby reducing overhead and increasing throughput.

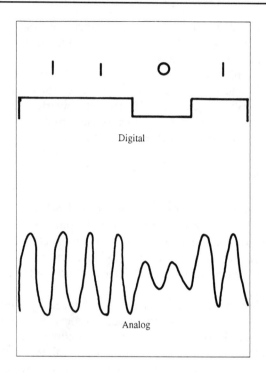

Figure 4.41 Digital and analog modulation.

Specialized modems are available for running Ethernet protocols over broadband, MAP (broadband and carrier band), or IEEE 802.4 protocols.

All broadband modems use frequency division to separate channels. In addition, they can use phase, amplitude, and frequency modulation formats. FM changes the frequency of the carrier but holds amplitude and phase relationships constant. In simplest form, a binary 1 is represented by one frequency while a binary 0 is represented by another frequency. FSK is a popular form of FM used in broadband modems.

AM systems vary the carrier signal (higher or lower) to represent binary 1 or binary 0 information. When a few discrete signal levels are used to represent the logical 1 and 0 states, the form of modulation is known as *amplitude shift keying* (ASK). ASK basically is an on-off form of keying. Any waveform has two sidebands. When AM is used with both sidebands intact, it is called *double-sideband modulation*. (See Fig. 4.42.) The information in each sideband is redundant, however, and it is possible to use a version of AM called *single-sideband modulation*, where one of the sidebands is clipped entirely. It has been the practice in the CATV

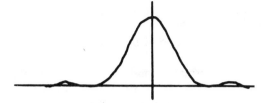

Figure 4.42 AM Signal.

community to use a modified single-sideband transmission format called *vestigial sideband* in which one of the sidebands is reduced but not completely eliminated. (See Fig. 4.43.) It sometimes is used in conjunction with phase modulation to produce *quadrature amplitude modulation* (QAM).

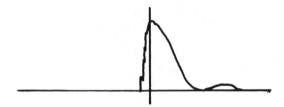

Figure 4.43 Vestigial sideband AM.

QAM can represent eight different bit messages by combining the two amplitude levels with four phase changes. QAM is more expensive than simpler FM schemes, for example, but is more bandwidth-efficient because it allows the sending of 3 bits for each single signal change state (baud). *Baud* describes how many times per second a signal changes its pattern (i.e., a rate of change of signal). Baud is sometimes confused with "bits per second," a measurement of data throughput. At low speeds, bits per second and baud are nearly identical. That relationship does not hold, however, as transmission rates increase.

Phase modulation alters the phase relationships of carrier signals to represent binary information. Think of a single complete oscillation of a wavelength as being a sine wave or circle. Each quarter rotation of the sine wave yields a 90° phase rotation. Hence, there are four possible phase states for each oscillation.

Theoretically, modems can pass idealized two-step waveforms with instantaneous transitions between the two levels used to represent the binary information. At high speeds, under somewhat noisy signal conditions or over longer transmission distances, however, bits exist in an environment where there are a range of possible levels created by random noise. In addition, transitions are not always instantaneous, and the bit widths may be wider than normal, a condition called *jitter*. (See Fig. 4.44.) *Overshoot* occurs when a transition from positive to negative continues past the level specified for negative before returning to the proper range. Overshoot can also occur when a transition from negative to positive continues past the set positive level before returning to the specified range. *Ringing* is caused by oscillations of the waveform that occur after a level transition has already been made. It is usually caused by impedance mismatches or improperly terminated ports.

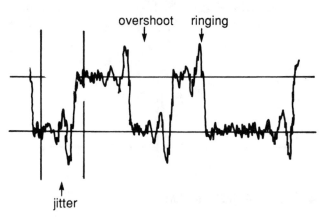

Figure 4.44 Jitter, overshoot, and ringing.

Several methods are available for formatting data before it is transported. NRZ represents logical zeros by a defined zero signal level, and logical ones are represented by some other signal level above zero. (See Fig. 4.45.) A switch to a new level, when required, is done at the start of each new bit. NRZ coding sometimes is referred to a *unipolar* coding. *Bipolar* NRZ does not use a defined zero state, but a positive level to represent logical 1 data and a negative level to represent logical 0 data. Biphase or Manchester encoding uses signal transitions occurring in the middle of a bit to represent logical 0 and logical 1 data. A 1 is represented by a high-to-low transition, and a 0 is represented as a low-to-high transition. Ethernet uses Manchester encoding. Alternate mark inversion uses a defined zero signal level to represent zeros but two nonzero signal levels to represent logical 1 data. T-1 systems commonly use alternate mark inversion.

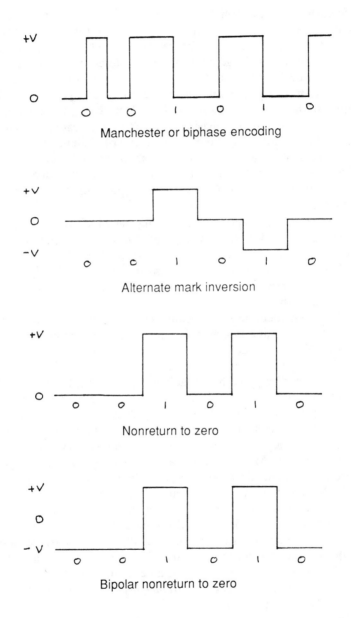

Figure 4.45 Digital coding methods.

Some modems, especially point-to-point devices, can be run independently of specific networks marketed by system vendors. Others are system-specific and designed to use frequencies and protocols required by proprietary networks. In general, modems offered by LAN vendors fall into three categories: (1) point-to-point, (2) standards-based general purpose, (3) proprietary general purpose. Some modems are designed to operate with the general-purpose LANs made by Sytek, Ungermann-Bass, TRW Information Systems Division, Bridge Communications, Computrol, Lanex, and others. Point-to-point modems can run independently of other network protocols so long as the channel frequencies do not conflict. It is possible, for example, to run Ethernet or MAP on a broadband network and to run independent pairings of point-to-point modems elsewhere in the spectrum.

There are LANs specifically running the MAP and conforming to IEEE standard 802.4 (token-passing broadband bus). Concord Communications, Allen-Bradley, and Industrial Networking, Inc., are suppliers of MAP-specification modems. There also are modems specially configured to run Ethernet protocols over broadband. Digital Equipment Corp. and Chipcom make them.

Most RF modems use AM techniques, sometimes in conjunction with other methods such as phase modulation. Catel Telecommunications, however, uses FM techniques, which require more bandwidth but provide better immunity to noise.

All RF modems used for broadband applications have in common a transmitting section, receiving section, RF modulator circuits, RF demodulator circuits, and a physical interface, such as RS-232. The transmitting section contains circuits that modulate messages with the intended format. FSK, ASK, or PSK are examples of common modulation formats. Modems designed to run on MAP networks also have a logic section responsible for decoding and encoding messages according to MAP standards.

All MAP data frames, or messages, begin with a *preamble*, a pattern of symbols that lets a receiver know the timing and amplitude information the receiver needs in order to read the data stream to follow. The first byte after the preamble is the *start-frame delimiter*. Its purpose is to separate the preamble from the message. The message contains the access token all stations require to transmit, a destination address, a source address, and the actual message. A *frame-check sequence* is appended to check for data transmission errors.

MAP modems also incorporate jabber circuits. (See Fig. 4.46.) Jabber circuits sense transmitting section error and disable the transmitting section if necessary. Many RF modems are run on contention access networks, where each modem on the network can transmit freely unless

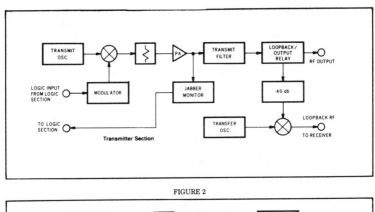

FIGURE 2

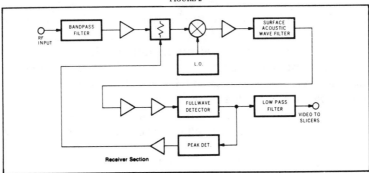

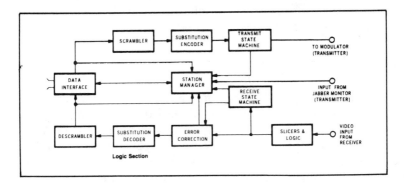

Figure 4.46 MAP modems. (Courtesy of Fairchild Data Corporation.)

another modem is already doing so. MAP networks, however, use a token-passing access scheme in which all stations have access to the network in set order, and no station is allowed to transmit more than a set amount of time before it relinquishes transmission rights to the next modem on the network. If a transmitting section were to fail (transmitting continuously without end, for example), the entire network would be disrupted. The jabber circuit is designed to prevent this type of error.

Jabber circuits automatically shut down any modem transmitting for more than half a second. About 500 μs are needed to pass a token, and 8 kb is the largest data frame MAP allows, so the jabber circuit is a way of detecting transmitter failure. Concord Communications goes one step further than the MAP specification requires when a modem is powered back up for network insertion. Concord's boxes and cards are interrogated in a loopback mode to see if the box is alive before it is put back on the network. Concord also is the only vendor to offer a transmitter enable function. Basically, the receiver has to lock to the headend before the transmitter is enabled. That feature is not so vital in a point-to-point application, but it is extremely helpful in a token environment.

Ethernet on broadband modems are different from general-purpose RF modems. Ethernet modems have the required RF modulation and demodulation circuits, but they are integrated with or attached to the Ethernet transceiver circuits that sense channel status ("no other stations on the line" or "line occupied"). The transceiver also generates and removes preamble bits appended to all messages, and transmits and receives packets.

RF modems have often been used in a multidrop mode where a master modem at the headend polls each of the remote modems in turn. The master modem can download global messages intended for all remote modems or pass along messages from other modems on the network.

4.9 INTERNETWORKING

Internetworking, the linking of two or more LANs to form a larger network, is an important topic for the broadband community, because broadband networks are increasingly being seen as backbone LANs to tie many different types of subsidiary networks together independently of the protocols and media used at the subnetwork level. Internetworking is both the connection of one LAN to one or more LANs as well as the connection of two or more LANs over a WAN or a MAN.

Four major types of devices and software are used to link networks, each operating at a different layer of the OSI reference model. A repeater (or amplifier) operates at the physical layer only and links two LAN segments using the same protocol but possibly different media (Ethernet over coaxial cable for one segment and Ethernet on fiber optics for another segment, perhaps). Repeaters join two network segments that are electrically joined.

Bridges are used to link two networks or segments at the data link layer or MAC layer. Bridges are capable of filtering and then forwarding appropriate traffic to the next network segment. Bridged networks are electrically independent from each other. A local bridge connects two or more directly connected networks, whereas a remote bridge connects LANs over some long-distance network or MAN.

Routers operate at the network layer and can only operate on networks using the same higher-level protocols. Routers must know the addresses of all devices on the network, and can be used to break a large network into smaller logical subsets.

Gateways are used to connect completely dissimilar LANs and must have the ability to translate all protocols used by either network at all OSI levels. Basically, data moving from one network to the other is run through the complete OSI protocol suite on one side before moving through the complete OSI suite on the other side. When LANs are connected over WANs, a gateway must be used.

Each type of device has its place. Repeaters are used to extend the distance a single network can cover. Bridges have minimal processing overhead but might not be as efficient as a router under certain conditions. Bridges do not, for example, have the inherent ability to detect the infinite circulation of a single packet on a looped network unless it has been equipped with loop-detection software. Recall that a bridge does not know the addresses of all devices on the network. It only knows which packets stay on one segment and which are passed to another.

Routers must be addressed directly by each communicating device and can choose the most efficient path for any message between two devices at any time. However, routers can be used only on homogeneous networks using the same protocols.

Gateways are essential for communication between heterogeneous protocols such as LANs and WANs. Because of the need for complete protocol conversion, there is much processing overhead involved. Consequently, the throughput of a gateway is not as high as for a router.

Chapter 5
System Design Issues

Broadband LANs are designed on the principle of unity gain. Simply, *unity gain* means that the amount of signal gain added by any single amplifier exactly compensates for the amount of signal loss in the preceding cable segment. (See Fig. 5.1.) Each cable segment is defined as lying between the previous amplifier's output and the following amplifier's input stage. The goal of unity-gain design is transparency of signal level. In essence, an entire broadband network can be thought of as a series of linked unity-gain sections. Ideally, signal levels delivered to every port on the network will be identical, thereby allowing for easy device relocation.

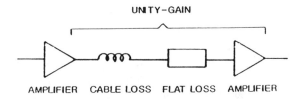

UNITY-GAIN

AMPLIFIER   CABLE LOSS   FLAT LOSS   AMPLIFIER

CABLE LOSS +FLAT LOSS =AMPLIFIER GAIN

Figure 5.1 Unity gain.

Unity-gain design requires trunk amplifiers that are identical (as far as the manufacturing process will permit) with respect to noise figure, gain, and equalization. In fact, each device response signature will vary a bit from the theoretical response. In addition, classes of devices will have group response signature characteristics: they are all similar to each other in the nonlinear response characteristics they exhibit. Unity-gain design also requires the use of identical lengths of cable between amplifiers to standardize the amount of signal loss. Recall that all coaxial cable exhibits a property known as tilt, the unequal attenuation of RF signals of differing frequencies. Higher frequencies attenuate more than lower frequencies. Identical lengths of cable allow standardized equalization of tilt in each amplifier stage.

Unity-gain design also requires that a standard size of cable be used consistently throughout the network. Trunk cables should all have the same dimensions. So should all drop and feeder cables. Since the electrical properties of a coaxial cable are affected by the type of dielectric material used in that cable (denser foam has different attenuation properties than a less dense foam or an air dielectric), the same brand and model of cable should be used throughout the network. In addition, *flat loss,* the amount of attenuation contributed by passive devices such as splitters, couplers, and taps, must be compensated by the amplifier.

Cable tilt also requires attention. Since cable attenuates frequency unequally, amplifiers somehow must boost signals unequally. That process is simplified by the use of equalizing circuits in amplifiers. (See Fig. 5.2.) Equalizers basically have attenuation characteristics that are the inverse of the cable tilt. An equalizer will attenuate low frequency signals more than it will high frequency signals. In a single unity-gain section, composed of a given length of cable, one amplifier, and the passive devices inserted onto that single length of cable, the equalizer will attenuate signals in precisely the proper amount to compensate for the tilt produced by the cable. That produces a flat output. A given unity-gain section might start out with a flat 32-dBmV signal level coming out of the headend. By the time the first trunk amplifier is reached, the signal level might be as much as 21 dBmV at channel 2 and 10 dBmV at channel 13. The equalizer at the amplifier would therefore have a slope, or differential frequency characteristic, that attenuates the channel 2 frequency 11 dB and the channel 13 frequency at 0 dB, the result being a uniform signal level at all frequencies of 10 dBmV. Lengths of cable often are described or specified by the amount of attenuation they cause. A length of cable might be described, for example, as a 22-dB section because it causes 22 dB of attenuation.

The operating levels of a trunk cascade will vary, depending on the length of the cascade, from 7 to 12 dBmV input to each amplifier. An input of 10 dBmV is fairly standard. Output levels are determined by adding the input level to the gain of the main station. If main-station gain is 22 dB, the output from device with 10-dBmV input is 32 dBmV. With a 22-dB gain amplifier, the maximum attenuation from all sources between one amplifier and the next is exactly 22 dB. The output can be flat, sloped,

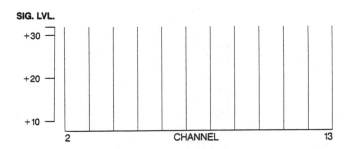

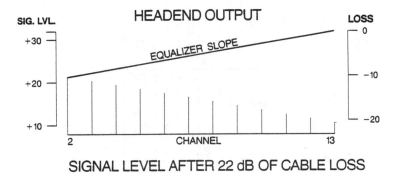

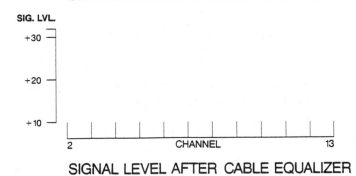

Figure 5.2 Cable equalizers.

or block tilted. (See Fig. 5.3.) Flat output means that all frequencies are at the same level. Sloped output means that there is a gradual increase in level as frequency increases, with a maximum high-low difference of 3 dB or possibly 6 dB. A block tilt means that the upper portion of the passband is amplified at a higher level than is the lower portion. A difference of 3

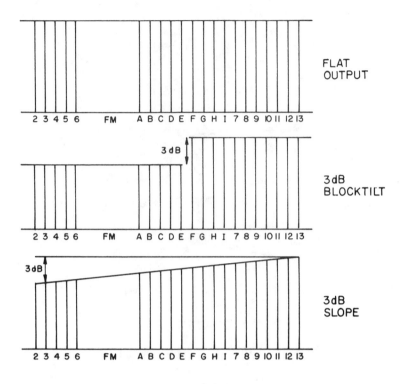

Figure 5.3 Amplifier output can be flat or tilted. (Courtesy of Magnavox CATV.)

dB would be common. In general, sloped- or block-tilted output is used for long cascades to provide better distortion performance.

5.1 REDUNDANCY

The actual distribution system (cable, amplifiers, headend equipment, power supplies) of a broadband network most often fails because of amplifier or power supply failure or physical severing of a cable. Some networks protect the integrity of the cable system itself by *redundancy*— that is, by running an active A cable while a spare B cable stands ready for activation if the A cable fails for any reason. (See Fig. 5.4.) To avoid a single point of disruption that would take out both cables simultaneously, we often route the A and B cables along physically separated paths. Even networks that do not use full cable plant redundancy typically have the cable located where it is unlikely to be accidentally cut. (See Fig. 5.5.)

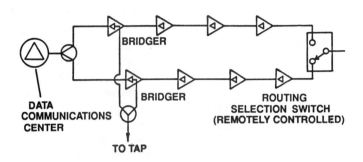

Figure 5.4 Diverse routing redundancy. (Courtesy of *CED*.)

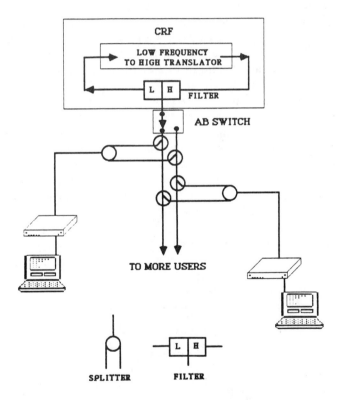

Figure 5.5 Redundant cable system. (Courtesy of C-COR Electronics, Inc.)

Of the active devices, it is the power supply that has the shorter MTBF and that is most likely to fail. A power supply can be said to have an MTBF of between 5 and 10 years. An amplifier, on the other hand, can have an MTBF of 20 to 50 years. Heat dissipation is an important factor in power supply life. Devices with good heat sinking tend to be more reliable than devices with poor heat sinking. Environmental conditions also play a part. Power supplies and amplifiers generate internal heat that basically "cooks" the circuits inside. That heat has to be dissipated, even more so if the supply or amplifier itself is working in a hot environment or in an area where there is poor air circulation.

Power supply redundancy typically is provided in one of two ways. Since the transformer is the most critical component in a power supply and is most likely to fail, a backup transformer can be used to provide redundancy. Alternatively, two complete supplies can be used, the first acting as the active supply and the second acting as a "hot" standby. Typically, an automatic default circuit switches to the backup supply in case of primary supply failure. An additional measure of protection is provided if the redundant supplies or transformers are further backed up with batteries that can operate from 2 to 4 h in case of a complete failure of commercial ac power.

Amplifier redundancy can be provided in several ways. One method is the use of redundant amplifiers. (See Fig. 5.6.) Typically, that can take the form of a spare internal power supply to convert 60-V commercial ac power to the 24-V dc power actually used by the amplifier circuits. Alternatively, or in conjunction with the spare power supply, it is possible to use fully redundant amplifier modules in a single housing. Typically each redundant set of modules would have an A/B switch with automatic switchover to the spare module in case of primary module failure. It is also possible to use fully redundant amplifiers in separate housings with automatic or manual switchover from the primary to the secondary amplifier. A passive form of redundancy is simply a shunt switch to route signals around any failed amplifier stage.

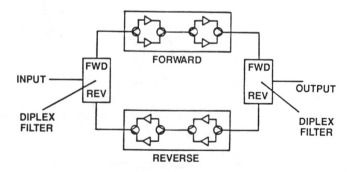

Figure 5.6 Redundant amplifier. (Courtesy of *CED*.)

To avoid even a momentary loss of signal, one also can design a system using two active amplifiers operating in parallel. If either amplifier, or a module in either amplifier, were to fail, the result would be a 6-dB lowering of signal level coming out of that particular amplifier station. Advantages of this method include ease of repair and that the operational amplifier need not be disrupted while the defective module or amplifier is being replaced.

5.2 BEFORE INSTALLATION

Typically, a user-needs survey will be conducted before actual network planning begins. It will be important to identify all existing networks in use, the operating software, throughput requirements, media types, access methods, and connectivity requirements already in place. Typically, different networks and throughput requirements as well as number of ports in use will be found at each work group or departmental site. The development of a frequency plan will hinge on what existing resources must be networked. The frequency plan also must encompass expected network growth in the future. Will additional network sites be added at a later time? Will video services be provided initially or possibly at a later time? Is the terminal or device user population expected to grow? If so, at what rate?

A survey of the existing base might probe for answers to the following issues:

1. What terminal equipment must be linked?
2. What types of traffic will the network be carrying (data only; voice and data; or voice, video, and data) and at what rates?
3. What access protocols are currently in use?
4. Is user access episodic or continuous (batch data entry, on-line access)?
5. How much time will typical users be spending in communication with other devices on the network?
6. Are there high-priority users who must be accommodated? Which users run applications that can be delayed if required? Which transactions are insensitive to network delay?
7. Are transactions typically short or lengthy? (Are CAD/CAM files being transferred, or is most of the traffic electronic mail of short message length?)
8. What application packages will be run over the network?
9. Is security or encryption required for any or all of the users?
10. What types of communication will be broadcast to all network users?
11. Which types of network traffic can be confined to the subnetwork level and which types of traffic must use the backbone network?

12. How much of the traffic will consist of downloading of files from central processors to terminals and other devices? How much device-to-device traffic will there be?

13. How many different buildings and floors of buildings will need to be linked together?

14. What is the peak, or maximum, throughput expected on the network?

15. Are frequent changes in traffic patterns expected? How many of the changes will be on a single subnetwork, and how many will require connectivity between users migrating to different subnetworks.

16. What type of communication will take place between users on the backbone network and other networks?

17. What type of throughput and gateway or bridge devices will be required to support network traffic?

18. Will the network gradually migrate to emerging international standards such as the OSI model? If so, will the network be compatible with those changes?

19. Where are existing computers and other intelligent devices located?

20. Where can monitoring stations be established?

21. Are users clustered or dispersed?

22. Are there sites that cannot be easily reached or sites where the cable itself will be endangered?

23. Are there existing ducts, conduit, or underground passages such as steam tunnels through which cables can be run? If not, can new conduit or duct paths be easily established?

Based on the results of the survey and a reasonable projection of future network traffic, an actual plan for frequency and channel use can be developed. Much will be determined by the types of networks already in place or which must be added. A MAP network, for example, will use at least one of three 12-MHz channel pairs: P/Q outbound and 3/4 return; R/S outbound and 1/5 return; or T/U outbound and 6/95 return. Depending on which channel pair is selected, there will be frequency conflicts with at least some versions of existing Sytek, Bridge, Ungermann-Bass, LanTel, DEC, TRW single-cable, Applitek, Concord Communications, Chipcom, or Allen-Bradley networks.

If multiple broadband networks will be run on the single network cable, the frequency plan must carefully avoid channel conflicts of this sort.

Channel nomenclature may be a bit confusing. MAP channel 4A, for example, used to be referred to as channel A-8. A recent channel designation plan adopted by the NCTA and EIA refers to this channel as channel 1. (See Fig. 5.7.) Similarly, MAP channel FM1 also has been called A-5. The NCTA-EIA nomenclature is channel 95.

Some thought also should be given to maintenance and operational issues.

1. Who will maintain the network?
2. Are additional network management personnel required, or can contract personnel be used?
3. What will it cost to hire and train additional personnel?
4. What management structure will be put in place to manage network resources?
5. Will there be a single network administrator or decentralized administrators?
6. Who will configure software for new and installed stations?
7. Who will perform backup of system files?
8. Who will monitor the network for error messages and network traffic?
9. Who will look for device or network failures and respond to them?
10. Who will initialize new nodes and maintain system security systems?

It also will be important to establish a frequency plan that will assign channels to the various services and avoid channel conflicts. Assume that a DECnet system and a Sytek system are in place and that the objective is to network both systems, as well as others, over a single backbone. In this case, there is no channel conflict. DEC uses the 54- to 72-MHz band for return communication while Sytek uses 72 to 108 MHz. DEC uses 210 to 228 MHz for outbound traffic, and Sytek uses 228 to 270 MHz. (See Fig. 5.8.)

On the other hand, assume that a DECnet is in place and the desire is to overlay a Concord Communications token-passing broadband system over Ethernet. Now there is a potential channel conflict. Concord uses the 60–96 MHz band for return traffic, which overlaps the DEC 54–MHz band. On the outbound portion of the network the frequencies do not overlap. If the single channel chosen for token ring return path communication is one of the two upper channel blocks (4A and 5, also known as channels 1 and 5; or channels 6 and FM1, also known as channels 6 and 95), there will be no channel conflict. Here, the need for frequency planning is quite important.

The frequency plan should take into account the channels presently used by existing networks or additional planned networks, the frequency split used by the backbone network (midsplit or highsplit) if a single-cable network is used, and the planned channel space to be devoted to other independent services (video, point-to-point services, voice traffic).

Frequency (lower edge)	New EIA/NCTA channel	Original channel number
5.75		T-7
11.75		T-8
17.75		T-9
23.75		T-10
29.75		T-11
35.75		T-12
41.75		T-13
54		2
60		3
66		4
72	1	A-8
76		5
82		6
90	95	A-5
96	96	A-4
102	97	A-3
108	98	A-2
114	99	A-1
120	14	A
126	15	B
132	16	C
138	17	D
144	18	E
150	19	F
156	20	G
162	21	H
168	22	I
174		7
180		8
186		9
192		10
198		11
204		12
210		13

Figure 5.7 Cable TV frequency chart.

216	23	J
222	24	K
228	25	L
234	26	M
240	27	N
246	28	O
252	29	P
258	30	Q
264	31	R
270	32	S
276	33	T
282	34	U
288	35	V
294	36	W
300	37	AA
306	38	BB
312	39	CC
318	40	DD
324	41	EE
330	42	FF
336	43	GG
342	44	HH
348	45	II
354	46	JJ
360	47	KK
366	48	LL
372	49	MM
378	50	NN
384	51	OO
390	52	PP
396	53	QQ
402	54	RR
408	55	SS
414	56	TT
420	57	UU
426	58	VV
432	59	WW
438	60	XX
444	61	YY
450	62	ZZ

Figure 5.7

Network	Reverse	Forward
Allen-Bradley Vista LAN PC	2-5	O-S
Allen-Bradley Vista MAP	3-A5	P-U
Bridge Communications	4A-A3	R-W
Applitek single-cable	T7-A4	H-Q
Applitek dual-cable	T13-U	T13-U
Concord Communications	3-A5	P-U
DEC	2-4	13-K
IBM PC Network	T14	J
Lanex single-cable	2-4A	J-L
Lanex dual-cable	T14-2	T14-2
Sytek LocalNet 20	T7-T8, 4-4A, A5-A4	K-L, O-P
Sytek System 2000	4A-A3	R-W
Sytek System 6000	T14	J
Sytek System 3000/7000	4-4A, A5-A4	K-L, O-P
TRW single-cable	T13-3	11-J, M-P
TRW dual-cable	T13-3	T13-3
Ungermann-Bass	3-6	P-T
Wang	T7-M	T7-M
Zenith	T7-T11, T13-4	M-Q

Figure 5.8 Broadband network frequency allocations.

Early in the process, a site for the headend should be chosen. Common choices are computer centers, PBX or telephone switch sites, the audio-visual communications centers, earth station complex, or a site in the middle of the enterprise to be networked. In some cases, it may be desirable to locate a main headend and several smaller headends that serve to break up the backbone network. Multiple headends also are a form of redundancy. If the main headend goes down, the subsidiary headends can be configured to replace it.

Cable routing should take expansion into account and use the fewest amplifiers to cover the distances and ports desired. Risers and existing cable trays should be identified where possible. Wiring closet locations are also important, as are any existing steam tunnels that can be used to run cable between buildings. If ceilings with drop panels are in place, the cable can be run above them at significantly less expense than running cable through walls.

Drop cable lengths should be as short as possible, so multitap placement is important. Try to put taps where a cluster of user ports is already located. Allow some margin for growth at each tap location. Some users have retained 25 to 50% of the tap capacity as a margin.

5.3 SIGNAL AND NOISE LEVELS

Transparency is the goal of broadband system design. Setting a signal carrier reference level and accompanying noise specifications is essential to maintain system transparency. The *carrier reference level* is a specified signal of amplitude at the highest frequency carried on the network. If, for example, the highest frequency is 400 MHz, then the reference level is set at so many dBmV of signal delivered to each network tap, measured at 400 MHz. Whatever the chosen reference level, the goal is to deliver exactly that level to the input of every device connected to the network. Two different video reference levels are used: one for receiving and one for transmitting. *Receiving level* refers to amplitude of all signals on the outbound path. *Transmitting level* refers to the amplitude of all signals injected into the system by any modem on the network.

A typical signal level for the receiver ports is 6 dBmV, which is the design amplitude expected at each modem at the receiver port no matter where that modem sits on the network. A typical transmitting level for all devices, whether the device is the headend translator, remodulator, or any single modem, is 56 dBmV. One might expect that total path loss from the headend to any given receiver port would be about 50 dB. Where does the 6-dBmV level come from? Recall that broadband has its origins in the CATV industry. The receiving level required by a TV receiver is between 0 and 15 dBmV. So typical receiving levels for that application have commonly run between 6 and 10 dBmV. The design objective was to put the actual receiving level at about the mid-range for a TV receiver.

These levels are for the RF carriers, however (see Fig. 5.9). When data carriers are used to subdivide a single 6-MHz channel into multiple data channels 300 kHz wide, for example, different amplitudes are required. Unless this were done, the modems could not differentiate between the main RF carrier and any of the subsidiary data carriers. If a single 6-MHz channel is subdivided into 300-kHz data channels, a total of 20 data carriers can be squeezed in. To determine the input levels for the data carriers, find 10 log (number of carriers), in this case 20, and subtract it from the receiving level of 6 dBmV. The receiving level for each individual data carrier would be 6 dBmV − 13 dBmV, or -7 dBmV. The group RF carrier then is 13 dB higher than the subsidiary data carriers.

The same holds for the transmitting level. A common transmitting level for a single data carrier might be 43 dBmV when RF carrier level is 56 dBmV. (See Fig. 5.10.) In general, the derating formula for figuring

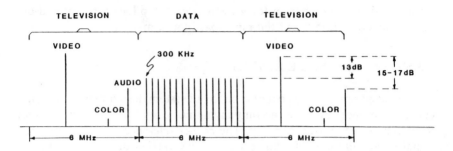

Figure 5.9 RF carrier levels. (Courtesy of General Instrument Corporation.)

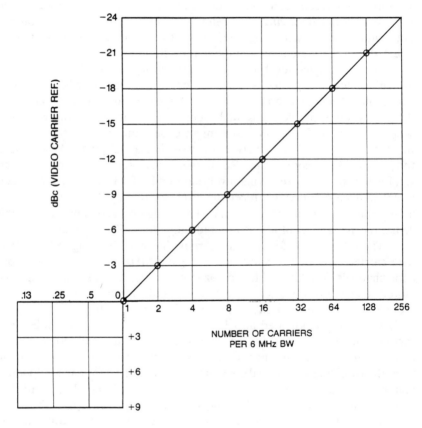

Figure 5.10 Data carrier levels. (Courtesy of General Instrument Corporation.)

out the data carrier levels is derived from the simple fact that as more data carriers are squeezed into any 6-MHz bandpass, less gain is available for each individual data carrier.

If 96-kHz data channels are used on a system with 56-dBmV transmitting level, there is room for 56 data carriers within any 6-MHz channel, each carrier having an input level of -12 dBmV. That result is derived from subtracting 10 log 56 from the receiving level of 6 dBmV. The transmitting level then is 10 log 56 subtracted from the transmitting level of 56 dBmV.

Lower *signal-to-noise ratio* (SNR) levels are possible when data carriers of such limited bandwidth are used, because noise increases directly with bandwidth: the wider the bandwidth, the higher the SNR performance required. The noise floor of a 300-kHz signal is -70 dBmV, and the noise floor of a 6-MHz channel is -59 dBmV.

A *noise floor* is the minimum noise level possible for any system operating above absolute zero. On a 75-Ω coaxial cable system operating at an ideal 68° F temperature, the noise floor for a standard TV channel using 4 MHz for the actual signal information is exactly -59 dBmV. As noted, the noise floor for a narrow bandwidth 300-kHz channel is -70 dBmV. The actual noise contributed to a system therefore depends on the noise floor and the actual noise figures of the devices on that system.

The noise figure of an amplifier, for example, is the amount of noise it contributes to signals it amplifies. A common noise figure for an amplifier is 7 dB, so the overall contribution to noise for a broadband system is the sum of the cascaded amplifiers. (See Fig. 5.11.) A single amplifier cascade using amplifiers with a noise figure of 7 dB would have a theoretical noise floor of -52 dBmV, the result of subtracting the 7-dB noise figure of the single amplifier from the theoretical -59 dBmV noise floor for a 75-Ω coaxial cable system at 68° F. As the number of amplifiers in cascade doubles, the system noise figure derates by 3 dB.

If another amplifier is added to the cascade, doubling the cascade from one to two amplifiers, the noise figure of the system derates by 3 dB. If the cascade doubles again to four amplifiers, the noise figure derates by 6 dB. If the cascade grows to eight amplifiers, another doubling, then the system noise figure derates by 9 dB. At 16 amplifiers the cascade derates by 12 dB. In general, a broadband system is designed such that the noise floor for the system is about 40 dB below the video reference (RF carrier) level. (See Fig. 5.12.)

Carrier-to-noise ratio (CNR) is the difference between the input signal level and the noise floor of a system. The rule of thumb is that CNR decreases by 3 dB each time the number of amplifiers doubles. Large broadband systems with long cascades of 32 amplifiers, -59-dBmV noise floor, 10-dBmV input signal level, and amplifiers with 7-dB noise figure

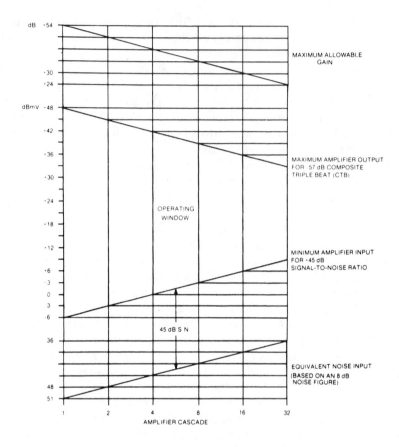

Figure 5.11 A typical system level graph. (Courtesy of *CED*.)

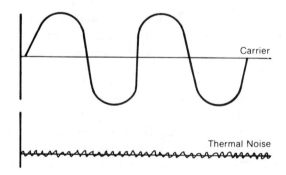

Figure 5.12 Carrier and noise waveforms. (Courtesy of *CED*.)

would deliver CNR performance of 47 dBmV, for example. The basic formula for calculating system CNR is to subtract the 10 log of the number of amplifiers from the CNR of a single amplifier.

A related measure called *carrier-to-hum ratio* (CHR) is a measure of how much hum modulation might be added to a system by power line artifacts. Recall that amplifiers are powered by ac current flowing directly on the cable at 60 Hz. Typically, a CHR should be 40 dB or more if possible. Each time the number of amplifiers in cascade doubles, CHR derates by 3 dB.

Intermodulation effects also must be taken into account. Intermodulation occurs when two or more signal frequencies mix, producing spurious products. Second-order products are created at sum and difference frequencies of two carriers. (See Fig. 5.13.) Third-order products are created at sum and difference frequencies when any three discrete carriers mix. *Composite triple beat* (CTB) is the sum total of all third-order beats occurring in a system. (See Fig. 5.14.) It is recommended that CTB, measured as the CTB performance of a single amplifier added to the 20 log of the number of those amplifiers in cascade, be 51 dB or better. The CTB is the number of decibels the beat products will fall below the video carrier level.

Knowing the number of amplifiers in cascade, noise floor, and required SNR and composite triple beat levels, one can construct a *system level graph*. The system level graph basically shows the limits which all amplifiers on the network must respect as far as input and output levels.

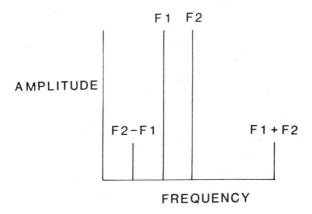

Figure 5.13 Second-order intermodulation. (Courtesy of Wavetek.)

FOR TRUNK CASCADE

$$= \text{CTB OF ONE} -20 \text{ LOG N}$$

FOR DISSIMILAR C/CTB RATIOS

$$= 20 \text{ LOG}_{10} \left(10^{\frac{CTB_1}{20}} + 10^{\frac{CTB_2}{20}} + 10^{\frac{CTB_3}{20}} \right)$$

NOTE: FORWARD & RETURN SYSTEM ARE CALCULATED
IN THE SAME FASHION

Figure 5.14 Distortion accumulation composite triple beat. (Courtesy of General Instrument Corporation.)

5.4 GAIN ISSUES

Usable amplifier gain is the amount of gain remaining after losses from any filters or equalizers are subtracted and a typical small margin of gain set aside to compensate for any signal level variations that might crop up when a theoretical system is translated into a real-world system. Common values of derating would assign about 1 dB for filter loss in any single amplifier stage and another 2 dB for equalizer-induced losses. The reserve gain could be as much as 2 dB. An amplifier specified as having 27 dB of gain then would be derated by about 5 dB, for a usable gain of 22 dB.

The signal level delivered to the input of each amplifier station is important. Higher signal levels will improve CNR performance but worsen intermodulation and crossmodulation performance. Lowering the input signal levels will improve distortion performance at the expense of CNR performance.

As we have seen, signals of differing frequencies attenuate differentially when passing through a broadband network. Lower frequencies are attenuated less; higher frequencies are attenuated more. Equalizing circuits are used in amplifiers to compensate for this uneven attenuation property of coaxial cable. (See Fig. 5.15.) Amplifiers sometimes are run with tilted output to compensate for the attenuation characteristics of the cable. But the signal level cannot be flat at every point on the cable span between any two amplifiers. It must be flat coming out of an amplifier, going into an amplifier, or at mid-span.

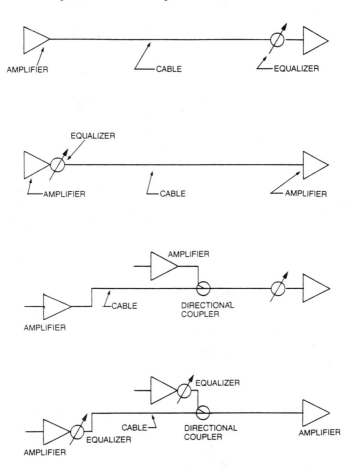

Figure 5.15 Pre-equalization *versus* post-equalization. (Courtesy of General Instrument Corporation.)

Flat output alignment is a method of setting amplifier output so that all frequencies have the same amplitude at the amplifier output. This method produces a flat response signature at the taps closest to the amplifier output. Obviously, as signals travel the length of the cable span, they exhibit increasingly uneven frequency response because low frequency signals are attenuated less than high frequency signals. It is a relatively easy form of alignment to perform. (See Fig. 5.16.)

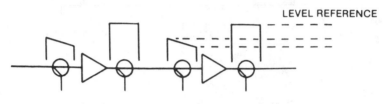

(a) Flat Amplifier Output Alignment

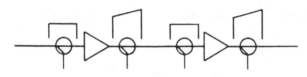

(b) Flat Amplifier Input Alignment

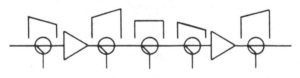

(c) Flat Midspan Alignment

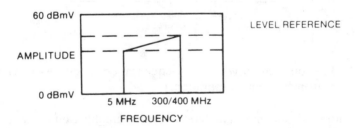

Figure 5.16 Amplifier alignment techniques. (Courtesy of *CED*.)

Flat amplifier input adjusts each amplifier on the network to produce equal input signal amplitude at every amplifier in cascade. With this method, response is flattest for the taps closest to the amplifier input in each unity-gain segment and most tilted at the previous amplifier's output.

Flat midspan adjustment produces maximum frequency flatness at a point halfway between the two amplifiers at either ends of a cable segment. This method produces the flattest response at the greatest number of taps between any two amplifiers.

Midspan flatness is a design goal frequently used by CATV operators because it maximizes the reach of a given cascade of amplifiers. Typically, trunk input levels are run lower than the midway levels to reduce distortion products. Distribution equipment, on the other hand, is run at substantially higher levels.

The process of checking for flat signal response for all frequencies carried on the network and equal signal levels at all network ports is called *alignment.* Assuming the system has been properly designed and all design specifications have been respected, the alignment process consists of measuring signal response for each cable segment and signal level at each user port. The alignment process for cable segments involves adjustment of the gain and equalizer controls at each amplifier stage while signal levels at drops are measured with an SLM.

Dual-cable networks need to be aligned only in the forward path. Single-cable networks must be aligned in both forward and return paths. The alignment process in the forward path generally involves the connection of a sweep signal generator (Fig. 5.17) in the headend to generate a reference signal and the use of a spectrum analyzer at downstream points, typically amplifiers, to recover and measure the spectrum. Return path measurements are similar, except that signals add as they flow back toward the headend. The reference signal is injected at the end of one or more cable segments, and the measurements are made at each amplifier.

Because signals add as they combine on the return path (every splitter in the forward path becomes a combiner on the return path), unity-gain criteria are difficult to follow for reverse path alignment. In fact, different losses should be expected from each cable leg because the distances covered by each leg are probably different. It is likely that gains will have to be adjusted at each return amplifier station.

Typically, a new network being turned on for the first time will be checked for RF emissions (leakage). A system that lets signals out also lets signals in. The usual method for checking is to use a leakage detection device. They have colorful names like Cuckoo, Sniffer, Searcher, and Tracer, and basically use a dipole antenna to pick up RF energy emitted from the cable and measure its strength on a meter. RF signal egress is usually caused by nonterminated drop cables, cracked cables, or damaged

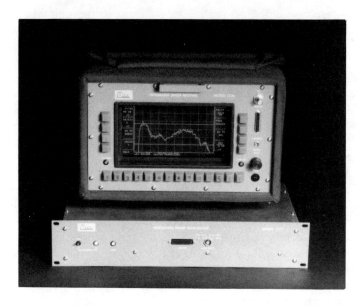

Figure 5.17 Sweep system display.

and ill-fitting connectors. In the CATV industry, which must comply with FCC rules for leakage, the standard is no more than 20 μV of energy per meter at a distance of 10 ft from any piece of cable. That works out to about -36 dBmV at channel 2 and about -46 dBmV at channel 13 frequencies. One relatively simple way to routinely patrol for leaks is to inject an FM signal onto the network at a frequency not used by any off-air FM broadcaster. Walking the system with a radio tuned to that frequency will quickly tip off the maintenance staff to any significant leaks. Other systems are designed to detect video carrier frequencies actually in use on the system and do not require the injection of a special test signal. (See Fig. 5.18.)

If any faults in the cable are causing impedance mismatches, the locations can be pinpointed by a *time-domain reflectometer* (TDR). The TDR operates on principles similar to radar; it injects a signal into one end of a piece of cable and measures any reflections that occur. The time it takes the reflected energy to return to the TDR pinpoints the location of the impedance mismatch.

Before a system is certified for start-up, it must be swept for frequency response. The desired system goal is flat response, meaning that all signals at all frequencies are carried at the same amplitude. The test to determine

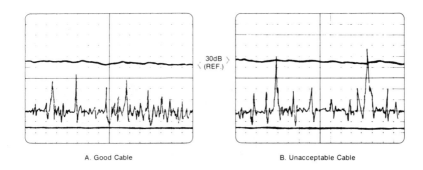

A. Good Cable   B. Unacceptable Cable

Figure 5.18 Cable frequency response. (Courtesy of *CED*.)

frequency response is called a *system sweep*. The equipment used to conduct such a test is called a *sweep system*. System sweeping and SRL tests are discussed in the next chapter.

5.5 TRUNK AND FEEDER DESIGN

There are several ways to craft the architecture of a broadband network. Smaller networks with few ports that must be constructed at relatively low cost can use a design called *tapped trunk*. (See Fig. 5.19.) In a tapped-trunk system there is no trunk and feeder cable system. Instead, all user ports are directly tapped off the trunk cables. These smaller networks typically can use LE technology. Slightly larger systems can use a modified trunk and feeder system based on high-gain amplifiers that are modified LEs. Since cascades are not long on a small-to-moderate system, the amplifiers can be run at much higher gains than are possible on a larger campus-wide network. Large campus-type LANs will use a traditional system architecture with trunk amplifiers on main trunk cables, bridger circuits to tap off energy for smaller distribution cables, and traditional LEs or LAN-type amplfiers. Broadband networks in factory or high-rise applications will use a riser layout that, depending on network size, can be a traditional trunk-and-feeder system. (See Fig. 5.20.) The difference is that, instead of radiating out horizontally, the riser system radiates out vertically to various floors of a single building. This riser-type layout is applicable to smaller networks using the higher-gain LAN-type or modified LE technology.

Some typical specifications for single-cable broadband network design might include a forward signal level out of the headend at 32 dBmV.

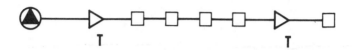

Figure 5.19 Tapped trunk. (Courtesy of C-COR Electronics, Inc.)

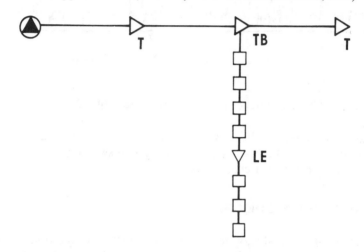

Figure 5.20 Trunk and feeder. (Courtesy of C-COR Electronics, Inc.)

(See Fig. 5.21.) Return signals might be specified at 37 dBmV. Outlets commonly are intended to receive 6-dBmV signal level with a tolerance of about 3 dB. They also transmit back to the headend at 56 dBmV. Response flatness should stay within 1 dB across any given 6-MHz channel and within 3 dB for the entire passband of interest in either forward or return directions.

CNR specifications for the forward path depend on the number of amplifiers in cascade. If only one amplifier is used, CNR can easily be set at 57 dB. With three to four amplifiers, CNR is satisfactory at about 48 dB. Between 9 and 15 amplifiers in cascade, 45 dB should do. In the return path, CNR should hold at 57 dB if only a single amplifier is in cascade. At three to four amplifiers, CNR still should be at 51 dB. At 9 to 15 amplifiers, CNR should be at least 45 dB.

Hum modulation should not exceed about 2% of the level of carriers. Second-order products should fall 60 dB below carrier level. The CTB performance should be at least 53 dB below the level of carriers. Any other spurious signals should fall 50 dB or more below carrier level. Although it is not strictly required by law, broadband systems should pass the FCC standards for leakage from CATV systems: less than 15 μV/m measured at a distance of 10 ft up to 54-MHz frequencies; no more than

	Forward	Return
1. Bandpass configuration 　　Mid-split bandpass 　　High-split bandpass 　　Dual cable bandpass	 156–300 or 450 MHz 222–450 MHz 40–300 or 450 MHz	 5–116 MHz 5–180 MHz 40–300 or 450 MHz
2. Headend Signal Level 　　(see Attachment 3)	+32 dBmV	+37 dBmV, ±3 dB
3. Outlet Signal Level	+6 dBmV, ±3 dB across, entire forward bandpass	
4. Outlet Transmit Level		+56 dBmV into network at the outlet.
5. Response Flatness (across any 　　6 MHz channel)	±1 dB	±1 dB
6. Peak-To-Valley Response	±3 dB	±3 dB
7. Carrier-To-Noise Ratio	45 dB	42 dB
8. Hum Modulation	2%	2%
9. Carrier-To-Second 　　Order Beats	−60 dB	−60 dB
10. Carrier-To-Composite 　　Triple Beats	−53 dB	−53 dB
11. Carrier-To-Coherent 　　Spurious Signals	−50 dB	−50 dB
12. System Radiation	FCC Section 76.605 (a) (12) 5–24 MHz less than 15 microv/meter @ 10' 54–216 MHz less than 20 microv/meter @ 100' >216 MHz less than 15 microv/meter @ 100'	
13. Outlet Isolation	25 dB between any two outlets at all frequencies within the forward or reverse bandpass	

Figure 5.21 Broadband LAN guideline specifications summary. (Courtesy of General Instrument Corporation.)

20 μV/m measured at a distance of 100 ft between 54 and 216 MHz; and no more than 15 μV/m measured at 100 ft from 216 MHz to the highest frequency.

Isolation between any two outlets on the network should be 25 dB or greater. Modems probably should be located no further than about 15 ft from the outlet (wallplate, usually).

In summary, recall that when signal levels are raised by 1 dB, CNR gets better by 1 dB while CTB gets worse by 2 dB. If signal levels are lowered by 1 dB, CNR worsens by 1 dB while CTB improves by 2 dB.

When an amplifier cascade doubles, CNR gets worse by 3 dB while CTB is worse by 6 dB. When amplifier cascades get to 10, CNR should be 10 dB worse than for a single-amplifier cascade and CTB will be 20 dB worse than for a single-amplifier cascade.

Chapter 6
System Operations and Testing

The RF carriers used on broadband LANs are the same as those used by TV broadcasters. Known as NTSC (National Television Systems Committee) signals, A TV broadcast signal is a combination of amplitude, frequency, phase, and pulse modulation formats using a 6-MHz bandwidth with a single sideband. A TV signal is, in fact, a composite waveform containing several different signals. (See Fig. 6.1.) A picture carrier, picture information, luminance (black-and-white information), chrominance (color information), aural or audio information, and an aural carrier are involved. (See Fig. 6.2.) Various synchronizing or timing signals are used to lock the TV picture horizontally and vertically on the receiver and keep the picture from rolling or having horizontal lines running through it.

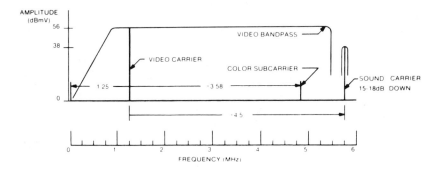

Figure 6.1 A typical television channel. (Courtesy of *CED*.)

Video information is amplitude modulated, and sound is frequency modulated. The vestigial sideband process reduces the bandwidth requirements for amplitude modulating the 4-MHz baseband TV signal. Conventional AM would require 8 MHz of bandwidth. It is possible, however, to

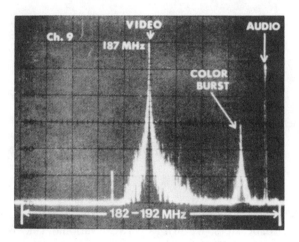

Figure 6.2 Display of one TV channel. (Courtesy of *CED*.)

recover all the information carried by the AM waveform from the carrier itself and a single sideband. The remaining sideband has a bandwidth of 4 MHz; the vestigial sideband has a bandwidth of 1.25 MHz. The visual, or picture, carrier is located 1.25 MHz above the lower band edge of the vestigial sideband, contains most of the transmitted power, and is used to transport and identify the actual information carried.

The visual carrier is basically an unmodulated signal oscillating at a known frequency. The video bandpass is 4.18 MHz, and the color carrier is located at 3.58 MHz above the video carrier. The aural, or sound, carrier is found 4.5 MHz above the video carrier.

A single waveform representing one horizontal line of a TV picture contains (see Fig. 6.3) the end of the previous horizontal line. The *front porch* initiates the next horizontal line and lasts 1.59 µs. Its purpose is to blank the screen of a TV receiver just before the beam starts its retrace from the right side of the screen to the left.

The front porch is followed by the *horizontal sync pulse*, sometimes called the *sync tip*, which synchronizes all sweep circuits in the receiver. It lasts 4.76 µs. It is followed by the *back porch*, also lasting 4.76 µs. The back porch keeps the TV receiver screen blanked until the next full line of picture information is transmitted. The actual picture information follows. In all, a single horizontal line of information is conveyed in 63.5 µs.

An NTSC picture is created by the painting of 30 frames a second of information on the screen of a receiver. For a single frame to be displayed, 525 separate horizontal lines are required. Like a motion picture,

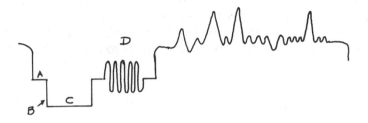

Figure 6.3 A single waveform.

TV signals are composed of multiple, serially linked still shots. If the frames are displayed rapidly enough, the illusion of smooth motion is created. In a motion picture, 24 frames a second would normally cause flicker. Producers get around that problem by flashing each frame twice. TV signals do roughly the same thing, displaying 30 frames a second and interlacing the pictures.

TV pictures are created by scanning an electron beam across the receiver screen from left to right and from top to bottom. During the retrace interval, when the beam physically is repositioned to the left of the screen and one line down, the picture tube is blanked out. When the electron beam reaches the last of the 525 lines, it must also be blanked out as it retraces from the bottom right of the screen to the top left of the screen.

Interlacing simply uses a weaving technique in which 262.5 lines of the first frame are painted on the screen. Because there are 525 lines and 262.5 is exactly half of 525, the scan ends in the middle of the screen. Then the electron gun is repositioned to display the information from the second portion of the full frame, beginning in the middle of the screen and continuing to the bottom of the screen. That takes care of the problem of flicker.

The actual baseband waveform which contains the information to be transmitted is mixed with a separate RF carrier before transmission. Typically, it is the RF carrier waveform that is the subject of most network testing and design principles.

6.1 MEASUREMENT PARAMETERS

Frequency, amplitude, phase, and the relationships among frequency, amplitude, and phase are at the heart of the measurements generally made on broadband systems. Accuracy of frequency reproduction is among the most important requirements for proper operation of a broadband network. (See Fig. 6.4.) If carriers are displaced in frequency distortion, interference can result. Bandpass filters may absorb portions of the sidebands and result in loss of the information carried on the sidebands. Signal accuracy is usually measured in hertz, percent of RF frequency, or parts per million.

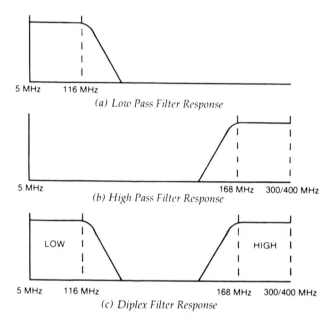

(a) Low Pass Filter Response

(b) High Pass Filter Response

(c) Diplex Filter Response

Figure 6.4 Filter response. (Courtesy of *CED*.)

Signal stability over time is also important. Signal sources tend to drift over time with age of the circuit, temperature, and presence of other variables, such as mechanical vibration or electromagnetic interference. A short-term change in frequency is called *residual FM;* a long-term change is called *drift.*

Signal level, or amplitude, is important because a certain level of power is required before a modem can distinguish a carrier from the background noise present on the network. Hence, an absolute power level presented to each modem on the network is important, as is signal flatness (Fig. 6.5), which measures how well each frequency in the passband of interest is reproduced as it moves through the distribution system. A flat system will show the same power level for each frequency at the end of a distribution system as at the headend.

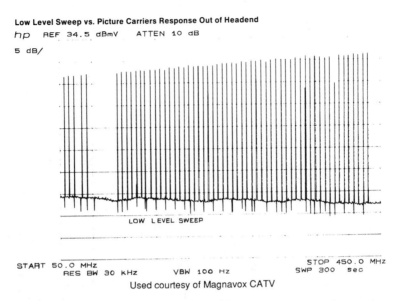

Low Level Sweep vs. Picture Carriers Response Out of Headend

hp   REF 34.5 dBmV   ATTEN 10 dB

5 dB/

LOW LEVEL SWEEP

START 50.0 MHz   STOP 450.0 MHz
      RES BW 30 kHz   VBW 100 Hz   SWP 300 sec

Used courtesy of Magnavox CATV

Figure 6.5 Signals should be flat. (Courtesy of Magnavox CATV.)

Thermal noise is an important amplitude parameter for broadband networks because it has all the attributes of a desired signal. That is, noise has a signal level and a frequency response pattern; it can be amplified, transmitted, and measured. When noise has enough power, it distorts or destroys the actual carrier information a modem needs to operate. Thermal noise is a background factor in an electronic device, but is boosted each time it passes through an amplifier in the amount specified by a device's noise figure.

Broadband noise measurements are always related to a given bandwidth, typically the 6-MHz channel. The wider the bandwidth being tested, the more noise power will show on the test instrument. Conversely, narrow bandwidths, such as those occupied by data carriers, will pass less thermal noise. Since most of the noise is contained in 4-MHz bandwidth, broadband measurements of noise usually are referenced to a 4-MHz passband. CNR (Fig. 6.6), the power difference between the RF carrier in question and the noise power density associated with that RF carrier, is a measurement of the difference in power between a video carrier and the system noise level at that frequency. If CNR gets into the 40-dB range, modems can experience problems.

Interference sources are both external and internal. External interference comes from RF signals in the atmosphere. A strong signal from a

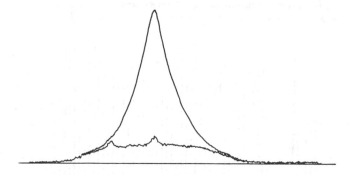

Figure 6.6 Carrier-to-noise spectrum.

local TV broadcaster is a typical problem when connector and cable integrities are compromised. Internal interference is most often caused by dc artifacts such as hum modulation due to the power carried on the cable. (See Fig. 6.7.) Internal interference is also caused by mixing of the various RF carriers on the system due to amplifier nonlinearity of response. The mixing of two channels on a broadband system is called *crossmodulation.*

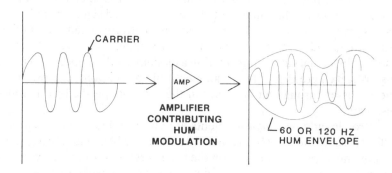

Figure 6.7 Hum modulation. (Courtesy of Wavetek.)

6.1.1 Decibels

Broadband networks cannot be designed or tested without reference to the decibel, a fundamental unit for describing differences in signal levels. Taps, for example, might specify 0.5-dB insertion loss between each leg of the tap. Two-way splitters might have 3 dB of loss between each signal path. Likewise, signal loss for 100 ft of RG-59 cable at channel 13 might be described as 6 dB.

An important related concept is the decibel referenced to 1 mV (dBmV). A trunk amplifier, for example, might have output specified at 33 dBmV output and 12 dBmV input, for example. These units of measurement are required to simplify calculations. The signal power at the output of an antenna can be as little as 10^{-10} W or as much 10^{-4} W at the output of a bridger amplifier. Such quantities are awkward to work with, especially when an entire system is being designed, requiring voltage calculations for every foot of cable and for every active and passive device on the network. Using dBs simplifies such calculations much as ratios can simplify measurements of length. If, for example, one wanted to know the relative change between the absolute quantities 100 in and 50 in, simple division (a ratio) would provide the answer 2. The quantity 100 is exactly twice the quantity 50. Decibels do the same thing. They allow changes in signal level to be described quickly, without reference to the actual voltage, current, or power levels involved.

Relationships between signal levels on a broadband network are always expressed in two fundamental ways, using the dB and dBmV. Sometimes the critical parameter is simply the difference between two signal levels, rather than the absolute level. At other times, it is more important, or equally important, to have an actual measure of absolute level. An example of the first case is signal level into and out of a tap. Here, the important measurement is amount of change. It is not necessary to describe the absolute level. The specification of a tap as a "12-dB tap" means that 12 dB of energy are taken from the cable and supplied to drop cables and outlets. This measurement is independent of the absolute level of energy available on the actual cable itself. This use of the decibel is a ratio, an expression of gain or loss, not a description of an absolute quantity of voltage, power, or current.

On the other hand, some measurement of absolute power is required. Hence, broadband engineers have adopted a reference value designated as 0 dBmV. This value of zero can be defined as 1000 μV measured across a 75-Ω impedance. (See Fig. 6.8.) This particular value was chosen because, at the time, it was considered a good voltage level for the input to a TV set. Any signal level measured in dBmV is so many times greater than or less than 0 dBmV.

The dBmV is always a measurement of absolute quantity compared to the reference of 0 dBmV. Any quantity less than 1 mV is expressed as a negative value. Any quantity greater than 1 mV is expressed as a positive value. Because the dB is simply a measurement of change while the dBmV is a measurement of absolute value, dBmV values cannot be added to, or subtracted from, dB values. On the other hand, dB values can be added to, or subtracted from, dBmV values. If, for example, signal level increases

dBmV	μV	dBmV	μV	dBmV	μV
-40	10	0	1,000	40	100,000
-39	11	1	1,100	41	110,000
-38	13	2	1,300	42	130,000
-37	14	3	1,400	43	140,000
-36	16	4	1,600	44	160,000
-35	18	5	1,800	45	180,000
-34	20	6	2,000	46	200,000
-33	22	7	2,200	47	220,000
-32	25	8	2,500	48	250,000
-31	28	9	2,800	49	280,000
-30	32	10	3,200	50	320,000
-29	36	11	3,600	51	360,000
-28	40	12	4,000	52	400,000
-27	45	13	4,500	53	450,000
-26	50	14	5,000	54	500,000
-25	56	15	5,600	55	560,000
-24	63	16	6,300	56	630,000
-23	70	17	7,000	57	700,000
-22	80	18	8,000	58	800,000
-21	90	19	9,000	59	900,000
-20	100	20	10,000	60	1.0 volt
-19	110	21	11,000	61	1.1 volts
-18	130	22	13,000	62	1.2 volts
-17	140	23	14,000	63	1.4 volts
-16	160	24	16,000	64	1.6 volts
-15	180	25	18,000	65	1.8 volts
-14	200	26	20,000	66	2.0 volts
-13	220	27	22,000	67	2.2 volts
-12	250	28	25,000	68	2.5 volts
-11	280	29	28,000	69	2.8 volts
-10	320	30	32,000	70	3.2 volts
-9	360	31	36,000	71	3.6 volts
-8	400	32	40,000	72	4.0 volts
-7	450	33	45,000	73	4.5 volts
-6	500	34	50,000	74	5.0 volts
-5	560	35	56,000	75	5.6 volts
-4	630	36	63,000	76	6.3 volts
-3	700	37	70,000	77	7.0 volts
-2	800	38	80,000	78	8.0 volts
-1	900	39	90,000	79	9.0 volts
-0	1,000	40	100,000	80	10.0 volts

Definition of dBmV: 0 dBmV = 1,000 μV across 75 ohms.

Figure 6.8 dBmV-to-voltage conversion chart. (Courtesy of *CED*.)

from 10 to 22 dBmV as it passes through an amplifier, the change in relative level can be described as 12 dB. But since the references are to actual signal levels, the 12 dB of relative change also describes 12 dBmV of absolute change in energy. On the other hand, dBs cannot be meaningfully added to or subtracted from a value of dBmV. The reason is simply that the dB describes the ratio of power, current, or voltage between two values without referencing the actual value. A 6-dB change, or example, represents a doubling of level. A 20-dB change represents a 10:1 difference in level. A 40-dB difference is a ratio of 100:1, a 60-dB difference a ratio of 1000:1. Simply knowing that a value has doubled or that the relationship between two discrete values is 2:1, however, tells one nothing about the actual values themselves.

Decibels are logarithmic (abbreviated mathematical expressions using powers of 10 to simplify calculations with very large or very small numbers). When using powers of 10, large numbers are reduced to values between 1 and 10, and small numbers are similarly increased. (See Fig. 6.9.) For example, 100 becomes 10^2, 1000 becomes 10^3, and 10,000 becomes 10^4. On the other hand, 0.1 becomes 10^{-1}, 0.01 becomes 10^{-2}, and 0.001 becomes 10^{-3}.

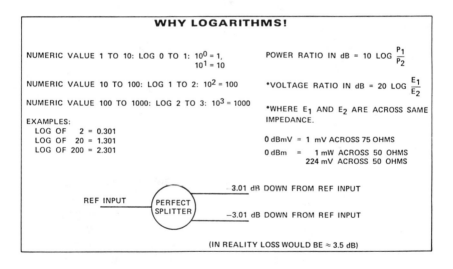

Figure 6.9 Examples of logarithms.

With logarithms, log 100 = 2 and log 10 = 1. The nice thing about logarithms is that multiplication operations become addition operations, and division operations become subtraction operations. For example, 23,000 times 7000 can be rewritten in logarithms as $(2.3 \times 10^4) \times (7 \times 10^3)$. One multiplies the integers ($2.3 \times 7 = 16.1$) and adds the exponents ($3 + 4 = 7$). The result is 16.1×10^7.

If measuring power, use the expression 10 log(power 1 divided by power 2) to calculate decibels. For voltage use 20 log(voltage 1 divided by voltage 2).

An important ratio is 6 dB, which represents a 2:1 ratio. When a signal level is doubled, the increase is 6 dB. When a signal level is halved (when emerging from a two-way splitter, for example), the level drop is 6 dB. A 10:1 ratio is represented by 20 dB, roughly the amount of gain produced by many trunk amplifiers. In the CATV industry 46 dB is roughly the lower CNR for delivering an acceptable TV picture to a TV set (45 dB is a typical bench mark). At 45 dB there is enough signal to overcome line noise, and roughly the same can be said for RF carriers on a broadband network. A common specification for maximum carrier-to-second-order distortion is −60 dB. A 60-dB ratio represents a relationship of 1000:1.

If only a single amplifier is on the forward path of any network leg, CNR should be about 57 dB. With three or four amplifiers in cascade on any single-cable run, CNR should be about 51 dB. At five to eight amplifiers, CNR should be at least 48 dB. Running 9 to 15 amplifiers on any single cascade requires a CNR of at least 45 dB. When cascades reach 16 to 20 amplifiers, CNR typically cannot be better than 43 dB. Return path CNR figures should be roughly comparable.

A typical figure for signal level coming out of a headend is 32 dBmV. Signals returning to the headend might be specified at 37 dBmV. At any port on the network designers will commonly specify a signal level of 6 dBmV. Each modem transmitting on the network might typically be expected to output 56 dBmV of signal level.

6.1.2 Frequency Response

Frequency response is one of the most important parameters a network designer will test for before the LAN is certified to be operational. (See Fig. 6.10.) *Frequency response* refers to the degree of flatness, or uniformity, of signal reproduction across the bandwidth of interest. A *flat* system is one in which signals at all frequencies of interest have the same amplitude. Deviations from perfectly uniform, or flat, response are measured by comparing the difference between the peak amplitude of the passband and the lowest amplitude of the passband. This measurement is known as a *peak-to-valley,* 0 dB being the ideal—virtually no difference in amplitude for any signal at any frequency. In practical terms, peak-to-valley is good if it is 2 dB on a distribution leg with 20 amplifiers operating to 300 MHz, for example. If the same network were operating to 440 MHz, permissible peak-to-valley would be good at about 3 dB.

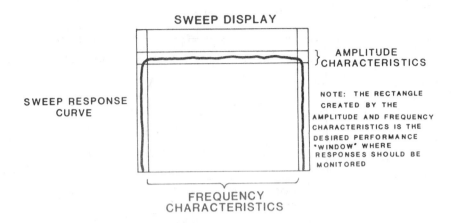

Figure 6.10 Frequency response. (Courtesy of Wavetek.)

Since system peak-to-valley (see Fig. 6.11) is largely a function of the performance of individual amplifiers, connectors, and cable, the best way to ensure total system flatness is to specify and maintain each component properly. Each amplifier and passive device has a slightly different frequency response pattern, known as a *response signature.* (See Fig. 6.12.) As signals are passed through successive amplifiers, lengths of cable, and passive devices such as splitters, taps, and combiners, the cumulative effect of the individual response signatures will affect total system response. A given model of tap, for example, might have a *frequency roll-off,* or drop in response, at either end of the transmission bandpass. Obviously, cascading several of these devices in series will produce a more pronounced

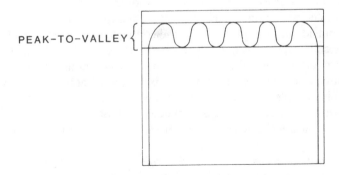

Figure 6.11 Peak-to-valley. (Courtesy of Wavetek.)

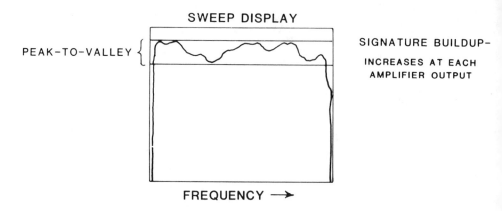

Figure 6.12 Signature build-up. (Courtesy of Wavetek.)

roll-off. Amplifiers have an individual response signature and a group response pattern, sometimes called a *ripple*. A cascade of identical amplifiers will therefore exhibit both the cumulative individual response signatures and the ripple produced by each of the units.

A common method for equalizing the response is to use controls in amplifiers. Amplifiers commonly can take modules called *response equalizers* (Fig. 6.13), which compensate for system frequency response. Usually a response equalizer circuit is located about every fifth amplifier in a cascade. If response changes dramatically between any two amplifiers in cascade, suspect problems in the cable itself or with connectors.

Signals between 50 and 300 MHz running through a 2000-foot length of 0.5-in coaxial cable can experience as much as 16 dB peak-to-valley. Transmission loss increases as the square root of frequency.

Poor connector response is usually caused by a loss of ground integrity through the outside of the connector. Loose connector fittings or corrosion are often the culprits; they weaken the electrical contact between the cable and connector or between the connector and its own housing. Another common source of poor connector response is loss of signal from the center conductor. This problem is commonly caused by a center conductor that is cut too short as a piece of cable is connectorized. Sometimes the center conductor is cut when the seizure mechanism in the housing is tightened too much.

Equalization, the technique of restoring signal flatness across the frequency band, is used to adjust for the uneven attenuation of signals of different frequencies as they move through coaxial cable. Simply speaking, higher frequencies are attenuated more than lower frequencies. Thus, an

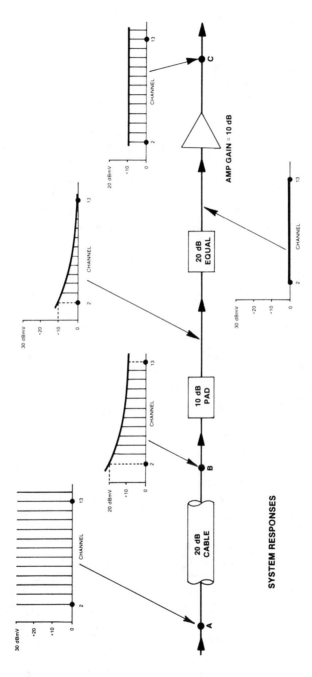

Figure 6.13 Response equalization. (Courtesy of Texscan.)

originally flat signal outbound from a single amplifier will have tilted by the time it reaches the input port of the next amplifier. In other words, signals will be stronger at the lower frequencies and much weaker at the higher frequencies. This characteristic of coaxial cable is known as tilt. Since the broadband LAN design goal is unity gain, or identical signal levels between each amplifier stage, the task of equalization means offsetting exactly the tilt in each cable segment by compensation within the amplifier. Unity gain means that the gain and loss in each cable segment negate each other. In other words, each amplifier exactly compensates for the losses and tilt introduced by the segment of cable that immediately precedes it. If equalization is attained, there will be no difference between signal levels between the input and output of each section of cable.

Of course, there is a slight issue to be resolved. A system can be designed so that signals are flat immediately coming out of an amplifier (flat output alignment), flat immediately going into an amplifier (flat input alignment), or flat halfway between two amplifier stations (flat midspan). All three are acceptable alignments. The point is that the response cannot be simultaneously flat at amplifier inputs, outputs, and midspan.

Passive devices such as splitters, directional couplers, or taps will exhibit response signature but not tilt. They instead introduce *flat loss,* attenuating all frequencies equally.

Network design presupposes signal level transparency throughout the system, so any deviation from flat frequency response may cause either insufficient signal strength or levels high enough to distort the signals on one or more channels. (See Fig. 6.14.) Active devices (such as amplifiers) and passive devices (such as cable and taps) have frequency response characteristics that are vital for system design and operation. In general, frequency response is so important because amplifiers are not perfectly linear. They cannot perfectly reproduce an incoming signal. In addition, the cable attenuates signals differentially. Higher frequencies are attenuated more than lower frequencies. Damaged cable attenuates certain frequencies more than others. Lastly, increasing the temperature increases the attenuation.

Coaxial cable technology, for example, has advanced through at least four different generations, and each generation has different electrical properties. Coaxial cable made during the middle 1960s, for example, was routinely swept for flatness (frequency response) from 50 to 108 MHz and 173 to 216 MHz, because those were the frequencies CATV operators could use. By 1972 CATV operators were using the 5- to 300-MHz bandwidth, and cable manufactured during the early 1970s was consequently swept for flatness in that range. By 1980 the usable bandwidth had increased to 450 MHz, so cable manufactured during the 1980s was routinely

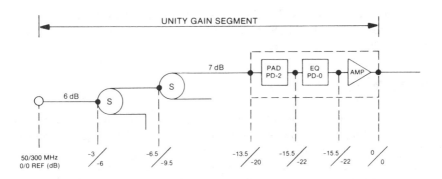

Figure 6.14 System unity segments. (Courtesy of Texscan.)

swept for flatness to 450 MHz. Beginning about 1984, bandwidth demands were again raised to about 600 MHz.

Early manufacturing technology had something to do with the frequency response of coaxial cable. It simply was not possible in the early days to make cable that was uniformly flat in terms of response across the entire frequency band. There were inevitably some frequency spikes, which generally caused signal loss in a relatively narrow bandwidth. Sometimes referred to as a *suck-out,* these spikes might, for example, have 12-dB response above 300 MHz, where the design goal was a uniform 26 dB of response. These spikes were tunable, however, so manufacturers of coaxial cable simply moved the spikes to frequencies that were not intended to be used. A cable certified to have 30-dB flat response from 5 to 300 MHz might very well have spikes above 300 MHz.

Even cable that is certified to be flat across the passband can be damaged during storage or shipping from kinking, being bent beyond its bend radius, or crushing. Such irregularities can cause suck-outs, typically at specific frequencies.

Early foams used as dielectrics tended to absorb moisture rather easily, leading to changes in attenuation characteristics. Present fourth-generation foams, however, have excellent moisture-blocking and moisture-resistance properties. Improvements in foam densities have also helped reduce cable attenuation. Earlier solid foams have attenuation as much as 36% higher than current gas-injected dielectrics. Intermediate generation chemically expanded dielectrics improved on the earlier solid dielectric and got attenuation performance to within 12% of current standards.

Many CATV operators using the older generations of cable have found that it simply cannot handle the higher bandwidths required of more modern CATV systems. LAN users will not have this problem, because all the new cable purchased today will have been swept to 600 MHz and certified flat to about 30 dB.

6.1.3 Testing for Response

The frequency response test is a measure of RF amplitude over a frequency range after the spectrum has been moved through a series of system components. The design and operational goal is to ensure that transmitted signals from any point on the network reach any other stations on the network at strengths great enough to be correctly received. A typical desired test response is that there be no more than 2 dB peak-to-valley across any 6-MHz channel. If a 12-MHz channel is used (for MAP or Ethernet, for example), the maximum peak-to-valley is often specified at no more than 3 dB. If an 18-MHz Ethernet channel is used, maximum peak-to-valley should not exceed 4 dB. If the desired response flatness is not achieved, it is possible that some of the amplifiers are not properly spaced, resulting in response signatures that are too high or too low. It is also possible that one or more of the passive devices is defective, or there might be unterminated ports causing reflections and impedance mismatches.

A frequency response or sweep test is an important measure of system flatness, and several methods of sweeping have been developed for broadband networks. The standard broadband and simultaneous sweeps (often referred to as *high-level sweeps*), the tracking (or *low-level*) sweep, and the slow (or *asynchronous*) sweep have been used for many years by the CATV industry. (See Fig. 6.15.) But they do have weaknesses in the LAN environment. They can cause bit errors or require that the network be shut down. A newer type of sweep, the noninterfering sweep, takes care of those problems. One should not assume that an interfering sweep cannot be used. CSMA/CD systems, for example, are quite tolerant of interfering sweeps. If a sweep signal collides with a transmitted message, the collision will be treated as any normal data collision, and retransmission of the message will occur.

Basically, all these tests compare a reference trace signal with the actual amplitude signature of the system. Equipment generally used for a standard broadband sweep includes a sweep generator to develop the reference signal, an oscilloscope to read the results, a detector to recover the trace signal, an attenuator, and an equalizer to feed the oscilloscope. This is an inexpensive way to run a sweep test, but it does require that the network be shut down while the test is in progress.

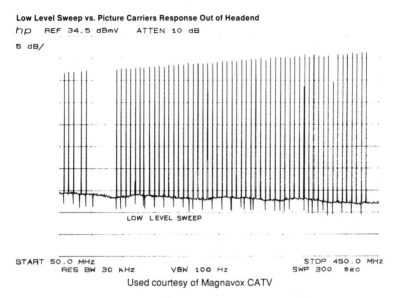

Figure 6.15 Low level sweep. (Courtesy of Magnavox CATV.)

A simultaneous sweep requires a sweep generator at the headend and a sweep receiver downstream (the receiver includes a detector, SLM, and oscilloscope) and can be conducted while the system is in operation. Simultaneous sweep offers superior resolution and accuracy because it inserts sweep signals 10 to 15 dB above video carrier levels, but bit errors may occur while the sweep is underway. (See Fig. 6.16)

A low-level sweep requires a low-level tracking sweep transmitter at the headend and a downstream receiver hooked to a spectrum analyzer. It works by injecting a sweep signal about 10 to 30 dB below the video carrier level. It does not require shutting down the system, and it produces relatively little signal interference. Resolution, however, is given up and does require a pilot signal. This form of sweep is widely used in the CATV industry.

The slow or asynchronous sweep is one of the most accurate methods and requires a sweep generator capable of conducting a slow sweep, a spectrum analyzer, and an oscilloscope camera. The generator is set up in the headend, and the analyzer and camera are set up downstream. However, this test does require that the network be shut down while the test is in progress.

The newest type of sweep is the noninterfering sweep. This sweep does not inject a sweep signal into the system itself but compares a reference signal at the headend with actual readings taken in the field.

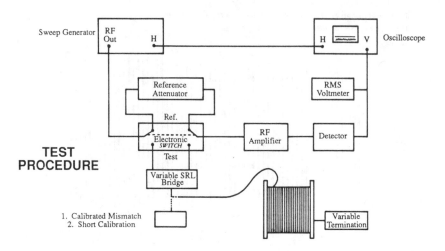

Figure 6.16 Sweep test. (Courtesy of Wavetek.)

Each test has advantages. The high-level sweeps offer greater resolution and accuracy and allow storage of the test data. But they can interfere with data transmissions. The low-level sweep is cheaper and produces less interference, but the results are harder to interpret. The noninterfering sweep offers good resolution and does not cause bit errors.

6.1.4 Distortion Issues

Amplifiers are not perfectly linear devices. That is, they cannot exactly reproduce an incoming signal but will introduce one or more artifacts, including noise, amplitude and frequency distortions, intermodulation or mixing effects between one or more channels, and harmonics (subsidiary signals produced at multiples of the base frequency).

All amplifiers contribute noise to the signals they boost. The amount of noise is called *noise figure* and is generally between 7 and 10 dB: the lower the noise figure, the better the amplifier. Amplitude distortion is caused by the nonlinear operation of the gain circuits. Each amplifier has a distortion signature, and, in general, every type of amplifier has a group signature as well. Frequency distortion normally is caused by the frequency-selective components used in an amplifier's circuits. Capacitors, RF chokes, transformers, and transistors, all have different frequency-shaping effects.

Generally speaking, a rule of thumb for CATV-type networks is that SNR has to be 43 to 45 dB or better. Both SNR and CNR measurements are used to describe broadband network performance. SNR refers to the relationship between baseband information and noise, whereas CNR refers to the relationship between the RF carrier and noise. For any given RF CNR figure, the corresponding SNR figure is about 4 dB lower. CNR usually is measured with a signal analysis meter (an SLM) or spectrum analyzer. If it drops too low, modems cannot discern the difference between the modulation and the noise, thus causing data transmission errors.

The noise generated in a single device is measured by figure and is related to a reference figure for a theoretically perfect device with a noise floor of -59 dBmV. A device with a noise figure of 9 dB would raise the noise floor to -50 dBmV. If the input to the device were at 10 dBmV, the CNR figure would be 60 dBmV. If the input to the device were 20 dBmV, the CNR figure would be 70 dB. The basic way to establish CNR for a single device is to add input signal level in dBmV to the noise floor of 59 dBmV and subtract the noise figure of the device.

System CNR is governed by the fact that power degrades by 3 dB each time the number of amplifiers doubles. Assume an 11-dBmV input level and devices with a noise figure of 9 dB. The CNR for a two-amplifier cascade is 58. If the cascade is doubled again, CNR for the system drops another 3 dB to 52 dBmV. For 16 amplifiers, CNR drops to 49 dBmV; for 32 amplifiers, CNR falls to 46 dBmV; and for 64 amplifiers, CNR is 43 dBmV.

In general, the trunk cascade is noise-limited because the input levels are lower. System noise will increase 3 dB each time the number of amplifiers in cascade is doubled. In contrast, the distribution system (from bridger amplifier to LEs) is distortion-limited. Because of the higher input levels, second- and third-order distortions will be much higher than on the trunk lines.

Harmonics are subsidiary frequencies at some multiple of a base frequency. Second harmonics are signals that are at twice the frequency of the original. (See Fig. 6.17.) The second harmonic of channel 2 at 55.25 MHz is 110.5 MHz. The use of push-pull amplification circuits that feed signals to the output 180° out of phase cancels the second-order distortions. Second-order distortion, on the other hand, cannot be eliminated by this phase-inversion process. Second-order distortion occurs when two or more frequencies mix with each other, or *beat* together, to produce new frequencies that are sum or difference products. Any two signals F_1 and F_2 interacting will produce distortions at frequencies $F_1 + F_2$ and $F_1 - F_2$.

Third-order products are created when two or more frequencies mix and produce third harmonics at three times the frequency of the base frequencies. (See Fig. 6.18.) Triple beat is a form of third-order product caused when three frequencies mix and produce new beat products that

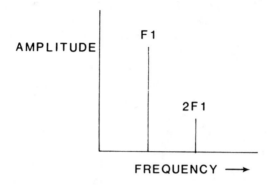

Figure 6.17 Harmonics. (Courtesy of Wavetek.)

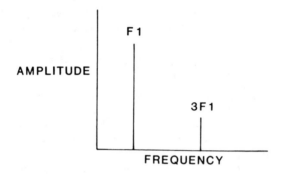

Figure 6.18 Third-order distortion. (Courtesy of Wavetek.)

are a sum or difference of the three frequencies. CTB is a measure of the combined triple beats of all frequencies carried on the system. Discrete triple beat is the measure of beat products produced by any three discrete carriers. (See Fig. 6.19.)

Composite second-order and composite third-order are the sum of all beat products produced by all the frequencies carried in the passband. It is a greater problem for CATV operators, who normally run their networks fully loaded, than for LAN operators, who run relatively lightly loaded networks.

Crossmodulation is a distortion product created when any carrier is mixed with one or more carriers also on the system. Crossmodulation artifacts increase at a ratio of 1:2 with increases in output level. If the

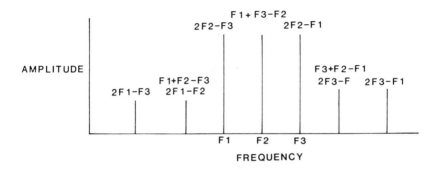

Figure 6.19 Discrete triple beat. (Courtesy of Wavetek.)

signal level is increased by 1 dB, crossmodulation increases by 2 dB. (See Fig. 6.20.) Also, every time the number of amplifiers in cascade doubles, crossmodulation gets worse by 6 dB.

CNR varies with carrier level on a one-for-one basis. If signal level increases by 1 dB, CNR improves by 1 dB. If signal level decreases by 1 dB, CNR degrades by 1 dB.

LETS RAISE ALL SYSTEM LEVELS 1 DB

WHAT HAPPENS TO C/N?
C/N BECOMES 1 dB BETTER (LARGER).

BEFORE   AFTER

Figure 6.20 Effect of raising all system levels 1 dB. (Courtesy of Texscan.)

CTB is affected by level changes and channel loading. (See Fig. 6.21.) Second-order artifacts vary on a one-for-one basis with signal level. (See Fig. 6.22.)

LETS RAISE ALL SYSTEM LEVELS 1 DB

WHAT HAPPENS TO THIRD ORDER DISTORTION?

THIRD ORDER DISTORTION PRODUCTS GET 3 dB LARGER. BUT, SINCE THE CARRIERS ARE ALL 1 dB·LARGER, THIRD ORDER PRODUCTS GET 2 dB CLOSER TO THE CARRIER LEVEL.

BEFORE   AFTER

THIRD ORDER DISTORTION INCLUDES
- CROSS-MODULATION
- SUM AND DIFFERENCE OF 3 CARRIERS ("TRIPLE BEAT")

Figure 6.21 Effect of raising all system levels 1 dB. (Courtesy of Texscan.)

Overall, the three distortion products that limit cascades are noise, CTB, and crossmodulation. CATV operators, running longer cascades, are very much concerned with CTB and crossmodulation. LAN operators, running far shorter cascades, should find noise performance a bigger concern than CTB or crossmodulation. Noise generally dictates the lower signal level threshold, and crossmodulation and CTB are the limiters in heavily loaded sytems.

6.1.5 Time-Domain Reflectometry

Return loss is a measure of how much signal will be reflected back toward a transmission source as that signal travels through a broadband cable. *Structural return loss* (SRL) refers to reflections caused by the inevitable mechanical irregularities that any cable will have as a result of the manufacturing process. Also known as *voltage standing wave ratio* (VSWR), it is a more general measurement of the reflection coefficient for a transmission line or device inserted onto the transmission line. Typically, return loss will be lowest for cable, moderate for passives, and

LETS RAISE ALL SYSTEM LEVELS 1 DB

WHAT HAPPENS TO SECOND ORDER DISTORTION?

SECOND ORDER DISTORTION PRODUCTS GET 2 dB WORSE
(LARGER). BUT, SINCE THE CARRIERS ARE ALL 1 dB
LARGER, SECOND ORDER PRODUCTS GET 1 dB CLOSER
TO THE CARRIER LEVEL.

BEFORE   AFTER

SECOND ORDER DISTORTION INCLUDES:
- SECOND HARMONICS
- SUM AND DIFFERENCE OF 2 CARRIERS

Figure 6.22 Effect of raising all system levels 1 dB. (Courtesy of Texscan.)

highest for amplifiers. Mismatches in cable might cause reflections that are 30 dB below carrier level, whereas mismatches in passives, such as taps, might cause reflections that are 20 dB below video level. Amplifiers might cause reflections that are 16 to 18 dB below video level.

Impedance mismatches, which usually are caused by unterminated ports, physically damaged cable, moisture in the cable, or corroded connectors and fittings, cause the reflected signals. It is almost impossible to prevent some degree of mismatch as signals move from cable to circuit boards or discrete components, or from cable to taps, splitters, or couplings. The reflections will not only cancel transmission energy but also cause distortion of the carrier waveforms and, therefore, bit errors.

Impedance is the opposition to an alternating current offered by a length of cable, tap, connector, terminator, or other device through which a signal passes on a broadband network. When all cabling and devices on a broadband LAN have exactly 75 Ω impedance, no signal will be reflected back toward a transmitter on the network because all signals generated by the transmission source are fully absorbed by the load. Whenever a mismatch occurs, however, some portion of the signal is reflected back toward the source because it is incompletely absorbed. For example, a cut cable has an impedance of infinity and reflects 100% of the signal.

Periodicity can affect the severity of reflections. If reflection-causing devices are spaced in such a way that they fall at odd multiples of the wavelength, the reflections may be out of phase and will tend to cancel each other. On the other hand, if the reflection-causing devices are spaced such that the wavelengths are even multiples, the reflected signals may tend to be in phase and hence will add to each other.

To ensure cable integrity, one should make an SRL test before drop or distribution cables are put into service on a broadband network. A TDR or variable RF bridge or sweep method can be used to check SRL performance. General Instrument's Comm/Scope Division recommends the use of the variable RF bridge or sweep method. The equipment required includes a sweep generator, RF switch and amplifier, detector, variable RF bridge, reference attenuator, variable attenuator, jumper cables, oscilloscope, and voltmeter.

The equipment is set up as shown, and a 30-dB reference attenuator calibration is made. The bridge is matched to the average cable characteristic impedance, and either sweep width or sweep speed is reduced (that gives the detector a better chance of producing response). With sweep controls set for full-scale display, the reference trace and minimums of the display trace should match.

If using the reduced-sweep-width method, reduce width to no more than 10 MHz. The entire bandwidth of interest should be swept in turn (10-MHz steps). Maximum reflections should not exceed the reference trace of 30 dB. The test is then repeated for the other end of the cable. If using the reduced sweep method, the entire bandwidth of interest is kept on the scope. Again, no spikes at any frequency of interest should exceed the 30-dB reference trace. The test is then repeated for the other end of the cable.

Wavetek Indiana also recommends the use of a sweep generator and display scope, return loss bridge, and fixed impedance bridge to test for return loss. Wavetek additionally suggests the use of an RF comparator to simplify the measurements. An RF comparator can toggle the sweep between the test device and a set of attenuators. Equipment required for the sweep-variable RF bridge method is made by Wavetek Indiana, Texscan Instruments, and Wideband Engineering, among others.

The TDR also will provide similar evidence of cable SRL integrity. A TDR uses a principle similar to radar—that is, it injects a signal burst into one end of a cable and times the arrival of reflections. A portion of the injected signal will be reflected back to the signal source whenever it encounters an impedance mismatch (which can be caused by physical damage such as kinking or flattening, poor connectorization, moisture, nonterminated ports, or cable breaks): the greater the mismatch, the greater the reflection. An open or short, for example, will reflect all of the pulse toward the transmitter. Lesser impedance mismatches will send smaller amounts of energy toward the source. The TDR times the return of the reflections and calculates the round-trip duration. Using the velocity of propagation time for the cable under test, one can derive the number of feet between the TDR and the source of the mismatch to within a few inches.

A TDR generally works with any constant-impedance cable using two conductors. Coaxial cables (75-Ω and 50-Ω typically used for broadband or Ethernet systems), twisted pair, twin lead, or flat ribbon cables are examples.

6.2 NETWORK TESTING

Loop loss, as we have discussed it, is a measurement of the attenuation of a signal as the signal makes a round-trip through a broadband network. Loop loss depends on cable diameter, composition of the center conductor, and type of dielectric. An SLM is typically used to measure loop loss. A reference signal is measured at a test point before a test signal is injected into the system. Similar level tests can then be made at other network test points and compared with the original reference level. Since a test carrier is injected into the system as a part of the loop loss test, unused frequencies or guard bands are the safest bets to avoid interference with network traffic.

CNR measurements are a measure of how well carrier signals can be received by modems on the network. It compares the signal level of the carrier waveforms to the level of noise on the network. The test can be performed using SLMs, spectrum analyzers, or specialized LAN meters with the ability to generate a reference signal. Test carriers are injected into the system, usually at both high and low ends of the passband of interest. Noise can be measured by tuning about 1 MHz off the center frequency of the carrier. Some test instruments will automatically correct for instrument noise. Measurements made on instruments that do not correct for instrument noise will need to be adjusted according to the tables supplied by the manufacturer.

Hum modulation is a low frequency modulation of carrier signals when the carriers move through devices on the network. The problem is often caused by faulty power supply filters or corroded passives. Many SLMs have built-in circuitry to perform hum modulation tests. Like many other signal analysis tests, the hum test requires a test carrier injected at the headend against which measurements taken at various network sites can be compared. If the SLM has a hum modulation test feature, all the technician has to do is tune to the test frequency and select the hum modulation test button. The percentage of hum modulation will be displayed on the meter.

Intermodulation is caused by the nonlinear response of amplifier circuits (harmonics, crossmodulation, and intermodulation). (See Fig. 6.23.) Some linear distortions are created by active devices, though. Distortion comparisons of amplitude *versus* frequency and phase *versus* frequency are possible. Second-order distortions, which are nonlinear, are produced when a circuit is run closer to the saturation point. The *saturation point* is a power level at which a circuit loses predictability of response. Third-order distortions caused by the mixing of three discrete carriers are a major issue in heavily loaded CATV systems, but not as great in relatively lightly loaded LAN systems. (See Fig. 6.24.)

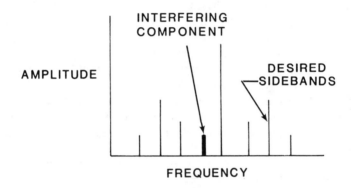

Figure 6.23 Intermodulation. (Courtesy of Wavetek.)

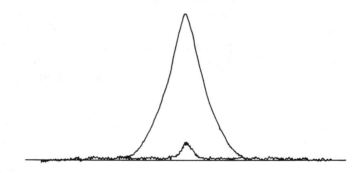

Figure 6.24 Composite triple beat.

The precise amplitude of the intermodulation products is not so important as the effects on given carriers. CATV operators have a bigger problem by far because their systems are heavily loaded with evenly spaced carriers using the same modulation techniques. The result is a buildup of third-order distortions. LANs, by way of contrast, typically are lightly loaded and may use a variety of modulation formats and carriers that are not so evenly spaced. Intermodulation tests require the use of a spectrum analyzer and a test signal generator.

A measurement criterion widely used for broadband systems is second-order distortion of 60 dB and discrete third-order distortion of 60 dB. A CTB specification of 53 dB is often recommended.

6.2.1 Status Monitoring

Status monitoring systems are used to monitor the integrity of the RF plant. Typical systems include transponder circuits installed within amplifiers and power supplies, at end-of-line locations, or at drop locations. Each transponder is polled by a computer at the headend for a variety of conditions. These would typically include RF levels inbound and outbound, transponder status, humidity within an amplifier housing, temperature within a housing, voltage and current supplied to a device, and housing open and shut status. A transponder is also able to control certain parameters, including A/B switch settings, enable-disable of the device or device alarms. Typical status monitoring systems allow setting of alarm condition tolerances, remote configuration of addresses, and updating of software.

Alarms might be triggered if the RF output level of an amplifier is exceeded, if the voltage or current thresholds for the device are exceeded, if the temperature inside a housing becomes too high, or if a redundant switch has failed. Alarms can also be triggered if the transponder has lost communications ability, if the lid to an amplifier is open, or if a transponder has failed or lost power.

Status monitoring systems used for broadband networks typically use an IBM PC or clone as a central processing unit and increasingly use graphical displays to pinpoint the location of out-of-tolerance conditions as well as alarm status.

Chapter 7
Broadband Systems

Completely broadband LANs are available from a few companies and fall into several types. Some broadband networks are designed to be general-purpose networks connecting a variety of devices (asynchronous and synchronous point-to-point connections, multidrop connections or fully networked connections, and terminal-host connections). Other networks are designed to run the MAP. Some networks are optimized to run Ethernet protocols, either Ethernet on broadband backbones or Ethernet on subnetworks communicating with each other over broadband backbones. Others use token-passing access. The players include Allen-Bradley, which specializes in factory-automation and MAP networks; Applitek, which offers both single-cable and dual-cable systems running a rather unique access protocol; Bridge Communications (a division of 3Com Corporation), which offers a single-cable system using the CSMA/CD access protocol; Concord Communications, a leading vendor of factory-automation and MAP networks; and Digital Equipment Corp., a pioneer of Ethernet-on-broadband implementations.

Sytek was an early CSMA/CD access broadband network vendor, as was Ungermann-Bass with its Net/One product line. It is unclear at this point whether Ungermann-Bass will continue to focus on general-purpose networks now that it has been absorbed by Tandem Computers (Cupertino, CA), however. Also up in the air is the company's joint venture with General Electric. Industrial Networking, Inc. (INI) is a vendor of MAP networks.

TRW Information Systems Division sells both single-cable and dual-cable broadband systems. Wang sells dual-cable only. Lanex supplies contention-based networks in dual-cable and single-cable versions. IBM sells the broadband-based PCNet, and M/A-COM offers dual-cable and single-cable general-purpose networks.

There also are several vendors of modem products that are compliant with one or more of the aforementioned LANs. Chipcom Corp. has a line of Ethernet-on-broadband products compliant with DEC's networks. Halley Systems is an established vendor of point-to-point and multidrop RF modems. EF Data, Fairchild Data Corp., C-COR Electronics, Phasecom, LanTel, Zenith, Catel, ISC Datacom, and Radyne Corp. also sell RF modems with various capabilities. LanTel and Halley offer voice modems in addition to data modems. Catel uses FM techniques that are more noise-resistant than the AM techniques typically used by RF modem vendors. ISC Datacom sells bandwidth-efficient modems using *quadrature phase-shift keying* (QPSK) modulation. Radyne has QPSK devices as well. Fairchild specializes in high-speed and medium-speed modems and MAP products. Concord Communications, Ungermann-Bass, and Allen-Bradley supply MAP-compliant modems. EF Data specializes in higher-speed products running at 56 or 64 kb/s as well as T-1 (1.544 Mb/s) and T-3 (45 Mb/s) rates.

C-COR Electronics recently has revamped its product offerings to offer much more flexible, frequency-agile devices in both synchronous and asynchronous versions. C-COR is stronger at the lower speeds: 2400 and 9600 b/s and 19.2 kb/s. ISC Datacom is stronger at medium speeds: 19.2 and 565 kb/s. Phasecom, which manufactured the modems that General Instrument Corp. once sold, has a line of products for the lower- to medium-speed market.

Sytek, one of the oldest broadband vendors, recently has broadened its product line in a way that illustrates where the broadband network market fits into networking at the local level. (See Fig. 7.1.) Increasingly, broadband is seen as a backbone architecture over which many diverse subnetworks can be unified. Bridges and gateways are the strategic products in this regard. Sytek offers several types of bridges: broadband-to-Ethernet, Ethernet-to-Ethernet, and Ethernet-to-token-bus-broadband. Sytek also offers a DDN gateway that allows an Ethernet system running TCP/IP access to the Defense Data Network (DDN), ARPAnet, or MilNet. The company's SNA gateway allows communication between PCs and SNA networks. A family of bridges also is available to connect the various LocalNet versions: LocalNet 6000 (IBM PC network), LocalNet 2000 (terminal-to-host), and LocalNet 20 (general-purpose broadband).

From its original position as a provider of broadband point-to-point connectivity capability for terminal-to-host applications, the company has grown to support Ethernet (both 50-Ω cable implementations and Ethernet-on-broadband) and PC networking options for smaller departmental networks. It has terminal-to-host products that operate in an ASCII (American standard code for information interchange) or IBM 3270 environment, and Sytek's PC networking products support TCP/IP protocols

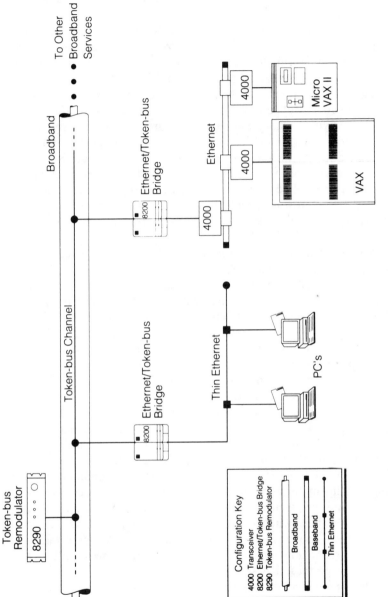

Figure 7.1 Internetworking is an integral part of Sytek's large network strategy.

and Novell's NetWare. Overall, the product placements reflect a shift in LAN trends in recent years.

Smaller networks connecting 9 to 15 PCs to shared peripherals have been the focus of the LAN market so far, reflecting the importance of the PC as a software platform. It appears that distributed processing clearly is the wave of the future. Novell, for example, talks about "PC centrism"— the building of networks on a foundation that has PC-to-PC connectivity as its prime objective. But corporate MIS staffs now wish to integrate these disparate LANs with existing computing resources to build a single enterprise network. Thus, multiple protocols must be supported not only because many differing technologies already are in place, but also, more importantly, users do not wish to be tied to a single vendor for all applications and networks. Therefore, internetworking (the linking of diverse LANs) clearly is a growing trend. TCP/IP's growing importance as an internetworking protocol is evidence of the importance of linking heterogeneous networks.

Another growing trend in large organizations is the increasing use of a mix of physical media within a given enterprise. It is rare that a single vendor, access protocol, operating system, or cabling medium is universally employed by all networks within a large enterprise. Some mixture of fiber optics, broadband, baseband, and twisted pair media will probably be the norm. An integrated, enterprise-wide network must have the ability to connect all of these media, and that is what Sytek has positioned itself to do. The company describes itself as a vendor of very large networks supporting (1) heterogeneous computing environments over a backbone and (2) various subnetworks running on different media.

Halley Systems, an experienced supplier of RF modems, has made internetworking the cornerstone of its corporate mission. (See Fig. 7.2.) Halley's new product line, to be called ConnectLAN, will focus on the building of integrated networks that provide transparent connectivity of LANs and WANs. These networks can be built on a broadband backbone employing intelligent bridges and routers operating at the data link and network level and interfacing to fiber optic transmission systems, T-1 carrier systems, or public-switched networks running X.25. The design is to avoid full protocol conversion and multiple interfaces. An important corollary is that graphically represented network management software is required to manage these LAN-WAN integrated networks.

Zenith Communication Products has taken an enterprise networking approach of offering a universal terminal-to-terminal, asynchronous-to-synchronous, terminal-to-host, PC-to-PC connectivity solution at low cost on a network running contention-based CSMA/CD protocols. The Z-LAN 500 system also incorporates gateways to Ethernet and X.25 networks.

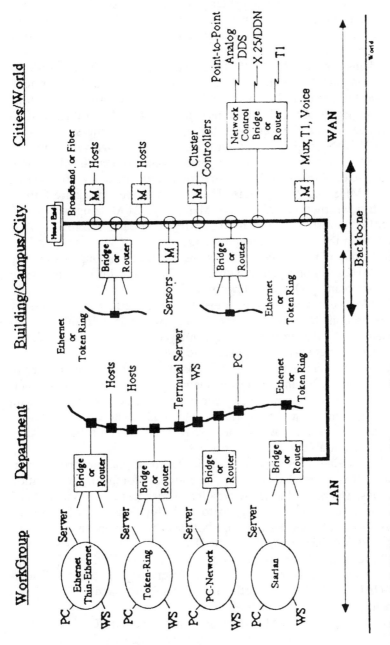

Figure 7.2 Halley's internetworking approach.

Z-LAN 500 uses both TDM and FDM to create four subchannels within each 6-MHz channel. The signaling rate for each subchannel is 0.5 Mb/s. Biphase shift keying is used to achieve low bit error rates even in noisy electrical environments.

Modems used on Z-LAN 500 are frequency-agile within a 12-MHz bandwidth and use the CSMA/CD access protocol and RS-232C interfaces. The physical interface to PCs is through a bus adapter card implementing the first four layers of the ISO reference model. The LANcard runs NET-BIOS. RS-232 connections are used for asynchronous devices.

The Z-LAN frequency translator can be set for high-split, subsplit, or mid-split configurations and is frequency-agile over a 30-MHz bandwidth. Six selectable channel pairs are used, and frequency offsets used are 192.25 MHz and 227.25 MHz. The upstream frequencies are 6 to 12 MHz with downstream of 234 to 240 MHz; 12 to 24 MHz upstream, 240 to 252 MHz downstream; and 24 to 36 MHz upstream, 252 to 264 MHz downstream in the subsplit configuration.

In the midsplit and high-split versions, the transmission pairs include 42 to 48 MHz upstream paired with 234 to 240 MHz downstream; 48 to 60 MHz upstream, 240 to 252 downstream; and 60 to 70 MHz upstream, 252 to 264 MHz downstream. One translator is required for each frequency pair in operation. If more than one frequency pair is used on a single-cable plant, a Z-LAN bridge can be employed at the headend to interconnect the two networks transparently to the users.

A network management console is used to control the operations of multiple networks. It can remotely configure modems throughout the network for frequency and power level, provide network diagnostics and data base management, adjust user access, and redistribute traffic when required. Zenith's network will surprise some users. It is a robust, flexible system offered at a very attractive price.

Allen-Bradley's network line includes baseband and carrier-band networks as well as broadband networks, all optimized for factory-automation applications. The general-purpose broadband line includes the VistaLAN/1 asynchronous network operating up to 19.2 kb/s (See Fig. 7.3) and the VistaLAN/3 802.3 network supporting both synchronous and asynchronous devices. VistaLAN/3 is compatible with IEEE 802.3, Ethernet, XNS, TCP/IP, X.25, ISO, and SNA standards and runs either TCP/IP or XNS operating software. The company's VistaMAP network supports MAP standards (IEEE 802.4) in both the broadband and carrier-band implementations.

Also available from Allen-Bradley is a broadband PC network running at 2.5 Mb/s and running Novell's NetWare, 3Com's 3+, and Banyan's Vines operating systems. Frequency-agile point-to-point modems also are

Figure 7.3 Allen-Bradley's 19.2 Kb frequency agile modem.

available that run at speeds to 19.2 Mb/s (150, 300, 600 b/s; 2.4-, 4.8-, and 9.6-kb/s speeds also are available). Five frequency bands are used: 216 to 222 MHz, 222 to 228 MHz, 228 to 234 MHz, 234 to 240 MHz, and 240 to 246 MHz. Each 6-MHz channel can be subdivided into 120 subchannels (60 translated pairs).

Recognizing the importance of the installed base of Ethernet LANs, Allen-Bradley includes as part of its product line an internetwork bridge that links Ethernets with the broadband VistaLAN/3 network, which has a radius of coverage of as much as 10 mi. A protocol transparent device, the IB/1 forwards internetwork traffic at a packet rate up to 2500 packets per second.

Bridge Communications has a broadband network running TCP/IP high-level protocols and using CSMA/CD contention access with a data rate of 5 Mb/s in a 6-MHz channel. Bridge uses a return bandwidth running from 71.75 to 107.75 MHz and a forward bandwidth running from 264 to 300 MHz. These bands provide the option of selecting any of six channel pairs for transmission. These pairs are 4A transmit (71.75 MHz) and R receive (264 MHz); 5 transmit (77.75 MHz) and S receive (270 MHz); 6 transmit (83.75 MHz) and T receive (276 MHz); FM1 transmit (89.75 MHz) and U receive (282 MHz); FM2 transmit (95.75 MHz) and V receive (288 MHz); and FM3 transmit (101.75 MHz) and W receive (294 MHz).

Bridge's broadband networks also use a single-channel remodulator at the headend that provides frequency translation and packet regeneration, filtering out in the process noise accumulated by carriers on the outbound and return paths. Nominal data receiving level for the remodulator is 0.1 dBmV, and data transmitting level is 52 dBmV. Video carrier transmitting level is set at 57 dBmV, and carrier receiving level is set at 6 dBmV. Dynamic range for modems on a Bridge network is about 30 dB, running from -15 to 15 dBmV with a nominal receiving level of 01 dBmV. Each Bridge modem has a jabber inhibit function that automatically shuts down any modem transmitting continuously for more than 3.28 ms, the maximum transmit time for any modem on the network. The Bridge network can be configured for either single-cable or dual-cable operation.

Configuration of large broadband networks operating or linking two separate broadband networks running on the same cable plant on different frequencies is accomplished by a broadband-to-broadband channel bridge operating at the data link layer. The bridge is used to create a single network on a large-facility campus where the distances to be spanned are greater than the 15-mi radius supportable by a single Bridge broadband network. The bridge also could link two separate broadband networks operating on the same cable plant but on different channel pairs. The broadband bridge actively filters messages by address, confining single network traffic but forwarding traffic with addresses on the other network. Local traffic is filtered at about 6800 packets a second while internetwork traffic is forwarded at about 3000 packets a second. If necessary, all six Bridge broadband network channel pairs can be used on a single cable plant by connecting multiple CB/1 units in series. The bridge operates independently of the higher-level protocols being run by the various networks (TCP/IP, Xerox Network Systems, or ISO, for example).

For networks running multiple Ethernets, the Gateway Server/6 can connect as many as 255 Ethernets over a single 6-MHz channel at a signaling rate of 2 Mb/s using CSMA access protocols. The GS/6 is frequency compatible with Sytek and Ungermann-Bass networks and uses midsplit and high-split frequency division. All local traffic is contained on the various Ethernet subnetworks. Only traffic bearing addresses on remote networks is forwarded. Transmitting frequencies run in 6-MHz blocks from channels 3 to 6 (59 to 89.75 MHz). Transmitting level for the GS/6 is adjustable between 30 and 50 dBmV. A 192.25-MHz offset from the transmitting frequency is used.

M/A-COM Telecommunications Division is another vendor offering Ethernet over broadband networks in single-cable and dual-cable versions. M/A-COM's frequency translator is designed for midsplit or high-split operation and accepts inputs in the frequency band between 53.75 and 71.75 MHz. It outputs frequencies in the 210- to 228-MHz or 246- to 264-MHz bands and is available with 156.25-MHz or 192.25-MHz offsets. Nominal output level is 56 dBmV, and nominal input level is 0 dBmV. M/A-COM's single-cable transceiver allows placement of any single node up to

1800 m from the headend and uses differential BPSK modulation. A single 18-MHz channel runs from 53.75 to 71.75 MHz. The dual-cable transceiver transmits over the 54- to 72-MHz bandwidth.

Lanex Corporation (Beltsville, MD) offers synchronous, asynchronous, and PC network interfaces for its broadband network. The company also has gateways to Ethernet and DDN networks and a broadband-to-StarLAN interface. The PC interface uses 802.3 access protocols running at 2 Mb/s on a single 6-MHz channel. For single-cable networks, five channel pairs are supported: 2 and O; 3 and P; 4 and Q; 4A and R. The frequency offset generally recommended is 192.25 MHz. The PC network uses FSK modulation techniques. On Lanex dual-cable networks the five standard channels used are T14, 2, 3, 4, and 4A. Other channels in the 50- to 76-MHz band can be used, however.

The IBM 3270 synchronous and asynchronous modems and interfaces use phase-continuous FSK modulation. Network monitoring functions available include display of any or all packets received by the monitor as well as cumulative packet totals. A connection map function showing which devices are connected to whom, and modem off-line status also is provided. The status and configuration of each interface on the network can be displayed on the network control console, and software updates can be downloaded to all interfaces from the console. Virtual circuits between any two interfaces can be created and removed from the console. For physical plant monitoring the C-COR status monitoring system is integrated into the management system.

An Ethernet interface is available for running Ethernet protocols over broadband on any of the five standard channels. For linking departmental networks of various types over the broadband backbone, a MAC-layer bridge is available. It runs 1500 packets per second for Ethernet to StarLAN connections, 2000 packets per second for Ethernet to broadband connections, 6600 packets per second for Ethernet-to-Ethernet connections, and 6600 packets per second for Ethernet to fiber optic backbones.

Lanex is a big supporter of TCP/IP transmission protocols and offers several software packages that allow devices of various types to communicate over a Lanex network. Among the supported CPUs are DEC VAX computers running VMS or UNIX, PCs running DOS, DEC MicroVAX computers running MicroVMS, and AT-type PCs running XENIX.

Concord Communications is a major supplier of MAP as well as general-purpose factory-automation networks using broadband technology and conforming to IEEE 802.4 standards. Concord's token-passing networks use the standard five channels running from 59.75 to 95.75 MHz for return path transmissions and the 252- to 288-MHz band for outbound transmissions. Interfaces to a variety of computing devices are supported, as is network management software and internetworking products. The

Series 4100 MAP bridges connect broadband and carrier-band networks, multiple MAP networks on the same cable, and remote MAP networks. Device interfaces are available for asynchronous and synchronous devices, IBM PCs, Multibus I systems, VMEbus systems, and RS-232C equipment.

The network management system for Concord's networks runs on an IBM PC/AT and provides status checks of packets sent, packet errors, number of stations on the network, and station addresses. The token rotation rate, total valid frames transmitted, modem channel settings, modulation formats, transmitting levels, and power receiving levels are all monitored from the management console. Report generation capability is provided for network configuration, monitoring, or diagnostic data.

Applitek Corp. sells single-cable and dual-cable broadband networks using a unique access system combining features of contention access with token-passing access, depending on network load. Under light load and bursty traffic conditions the UniLINK access protocol acts like CSMA/CD. As load builds, though, UniLINK switches to token-passing access when traffic builds or intelligent synchronous devices are added. Intensive CAD/CAM applications or situations where network size results in communicating stations being more than 5 mi apart also call for the token access mode. CSMA/CD is better suited to nonintelligent, asynchronous terminal traffic, distances less than 5 mi, and bursty communications with variable transmission delay. Token access, by way of contrast, is better for intelligent terminal communications, large file transfers, synchronous traffic, regular message traffic, or fixed message length traffic.

Applitek also supports Ethernet access protocols on baseband, broadband, or fiber optic media. A single 6-MHz channel is used for the broadband version. The frequency-agile broadband modem uses QPSK modulation and runs at 10 Mb/s in the 20- to 375-MHz frequency range. It accommodates any frequency split and also can be used on dual-cable systems. MAP and Ethernet modems have a jabber inhibit function that automatically disables any modem transmitting more than a fixed length of time. UniLAN modems have a similar function called "blabbermouth" control that does the same thing. The broadband modem comes in a circuit board form, and it transmits at 55 dBmV and receives at 6 dBmV.

The company supports DEC VAX and PDP-11, Gould, Harris, Apollo, and Sun hosts, among others. In the synchronous area UniLAN supports IBM's SDLC and BSC controllers, Sperry UNIVAC, and Burroughs controllers. Honeywell host-to-BSC controllers and Honeywell host-to-asynchronous terminals are also supported. CDC, NCR Tower, SUN Microsystems, or Apollo host-to-asynchronous terminal communication all are provided for by the terminal connection hardware and software.

The company's bridge and gateway line provides connectivity for heterogeneous networks and LAN-to-LAN and LAN-to-WAN networking. Ethernet, T-1, and interchannel bridges are part of the line. The Ethernet bridge can be used to connect Ethernets over a UniLAN backbone. The T-1 bridge connects UniLANs over T-1 links. The interchannel bridges are used to connect multiple UniLAN networks operating on different frequencies. Intermedia bridges are used to connect multiple UniLANs running on different media (broadband cabling, baseband coaxial cable, or fiber optic cable). Gateway products are used to link SNA hosts as well as UniLANs and X.25 networks.

WangNet is a dual-cable broadband network originally developed more as a connectivity solution for Wang computers than as a general-purpose LAN, but it does provide five service bands providing communication services between Wang processors, Wang processors to Wang terminals, multivendor services, Wang PCs, and seven dedicated video channels. The multivendor service band supports a variety of connectivity options, including general-purpose terminal-to-host connections, 802.3, and IBM PC Network. Asynchronous links using RS-232 or V.24 pins can run from 50 b/s to 19.2 kb/s. Point-to-point connections can run at 5 Mb/s using the CSMA access protocol. Dedicated point-to-point or multidrop links can be run at speeds up to 9.6 kb/s. In addition, the multivendor band sets aside five Ethernet channels.

FastLAN is the modular packaging of WangNet and includes amplifiers, splitters, drops, outlets, and precut cable. It is designed to allow user installation without the need for balancing and certification. FastLAN A is an amplifier box that controls signal and noise levels on the network; a maximum of five may be used on a single FastLAN. FastLAN B includes two coupler boxes, each of which can take four drops and support two more branches. FastLAN C is a drop cable and four-port outlet. Fully deployed, a FastLAN can support 640 nodes. Many users configure multiple FastLANs to create larger networks.

Ungermann-Bass, an independent firm recently acquired by Tandem Computers, has offered general-purpose Ethernet LANs running on broadband, fiber optic, and baseband cabling since July 1981. The Net/One system comes in five versions: a 10-Mb/s Ethernet-compatible baseband version, a 10-Mb/s thin coaxial cable version, a 5-Mb/s broadband version, an Ethernet-compatible fiber optic system, and a 4-Mb/s 802.5 token ring version. In conjunction with General Electric Co., Ungermann-Bass also is a partner in Industrial Networking, Inc., which develops networks conforming to the MAP. In addition to its network management software, Ungermann-Bass also supplies a variety of local and remote bridges, IBM 3270 environment connections, and X.25 connections.

TRW Information Networks Division markets the TRW Concept 2000, a general-purpose network running on a single or dual cable and running CSMA access protocols between 5 and 450 MHz. Linking of departmental PC networks and Ethernet subnetworks connected over the broadband backbone all are capabilities built into the Concept 2000 product line. High-split and midsplit options are supported, and the network monitor is based on a DEC PDP-11/23. It monitors modem operation and cable plant status. The operating system runs on a DEC VAX.

Chipcom Corp. specializes in products running Ethernet over broadband. Its Ethermodem line includes a headend remodulator and a translator and various modem products. The Ethermodem III/12, for example, is a modular product running in a 12-MHz bandwidth that allows simultaneous use of an additional Ethernet and a MAP system on the same cable.

LanTel Corp. produces translators, data, and voice modems in both synchronous and asynchronous versions, running at 156.25-MHz or 168.25-MHz frequency offsets. Transmission speeds run to 19.2 kb/s. If a user is looking for voice and telephone applications over broadband, LanTel is just about the only vendor in the market. Halley Systems offers digitized point-to-point voice applications. Switched voice applications are available only from LanTel.

ISC Datacom specializes in broadband modems and microwave products. Its two current offerings are the Model 1056 modem running at 56 kb/s and the Model 1019 modem running at 19.2 kb/s. Both use spectrum-efficient QPSK modulation. The Model 1019 can accommodate 2650 data channels, and the faster Model 1056 supports up to 662 channels.

EF Data Corp. builds satellite and broadband modems and a frequency translator that is frequency-agile between 5 and 400 MHz (it supports the standard 156.25- and 192.25-MHz offsets along with any other custom configuration). The company specializes in high-speed modems, such as the BCM-101/T1, which supports T-1 speeds. The BCM-101/SDR runs at any speed between 200 kb/s and 6.3 Mb/s. The BCM-64 runs at 56 and 64 kb/s.

Fairchild Data Corp. also builds satellite and broadband modems and makes MAP modems that are board-level products.

APPENDICES

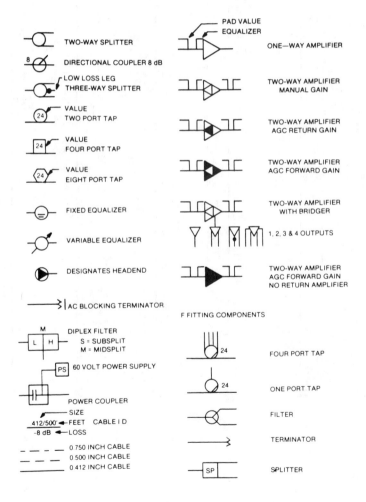

Appendix A Broadband symbols. (Courtesy of *CED*.)

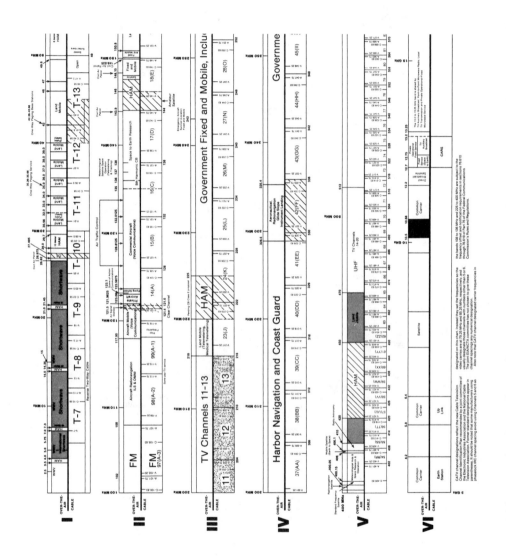

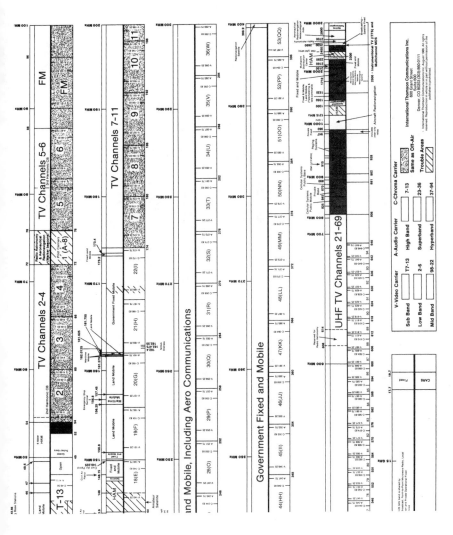

Appendix B Frequency allocation chart. (Courtesy of International Thomson Communications, Inc.)

GLOSSARY

ac—Alternating current is a flow of electricity that reaches a maximum in one direction, decreases to zero, and then reaches a maximum again as it flows in the opposite direction.

Active device—Any device or circuit on a broadband LAN requiring the use of electrical power to operate.

Alternate mark encoding—A signal representation scheme using zero signals to represent negative information and nonzero signal levels to represent positive information.

Amplifier—An electronic device operating as a repeater on a broadband LAN to repeat and strengthen signals.

Amplitude modulation (AM)—A way of expressing information by varying the amplitude of a carrier wave.

Amplitude shift keying (ASK)—A form of amplitude modulation that shifts the amplitude of the carrier among a few discrete levels.

Asynchronous transmission—A form of data communications in which there is no common bit stream synchronization between sending and receiving terminal in time. No common clocking mechanism is used. Instead start and stop bits are used to separate packets.

Attenuation—The decrease in amplitude of signals traveling through a broadband network, caused by coaxial cable and other active and passive devices on the network.

Automatic gain control (AGC)—An electronic circuit in an amplifier that can compensate for variances in signal level on an amplifier's input such that the output level is always held constant. It is sometimes known as automatic level control.

Automatic slope control (ASC)—An electronic circuit in an amplifier that corrects for the uneven attenuation of RF signals at different frequencies as they pass through coaxial cable. Known as "tilt," coaxial cable attenuates higher frequencies more than lower frequencies.

Automatic temperature control—An electronic circuit in an amplifier that can change gain settings depending on the ambient temperature.

Backbone—The trunk system used by a multimedia LAN to connect various subnetworks, generally at high data rates over enterprise-wide distances.

Bandpass filter—A circuit that permits desired signals within a certain frequency range to pass through, but traps all signals outside that frequency range.

Bandwidth—The carrying capacity of a medium as measured by the number of kilohertz or megahertz it can pass.

Baseband—A single-channel signaling technique in which the digital information is directly impressed onto the physical medium without use of a carrier.

Baud—A measure of signaling speed on a network commonly confused with bits per second. Baud refers to the number of symbols that can be transferred in 1 s, no matter how many bits are represented by each symbol.

Beats—Undesired subsidiary waveforms created by the mixing of desired frequencies as they are passed through an amplifier circuit.

Bridge—Software and hardware used to connect two LANs using the same logical link control but possibly different medium access controls.

Bridger—An amplifier used to tap RF energy off a trunk line and feed it to a distribution network of line extenders.

Broadband—An RF transmission technique using 75-Ω coaxial cable and standard CATV industry components. Broadband signaling requires the use of RF carriers to transport baseband information, which can consist of data, video, or voice signals.

Bus—A network topology in which all nodes are directly connected to a single strand of cabling. Ethernet is a bus topology. Broadband networks use a variant of bus topology known as *tree* topology, in which all network branches radiate out from a common point known as the headend.

Carrier band—A single-channel broadband signaling technique used by the manufacturing automation protocol.

CATV—An acronym for community antenna television, the name cable television technology was first known by.

Channel—On broadband networks, a channel is a 6-MHz-wide frequency band corresponding to a single TV channel.

Channel capacity—The maximum number of 6-MHz channels a broadband network can carry.

Characteristic impedance—The typical impedance, or electrical resistance, presented to signals traveling through cable or devices. The characteristic impedance for broadband networks is 75 Ω. IEEE 802.3 and Ethernet systems use components with 50-Ω impedance.

Cheapernet—An IEEE 802.3 standard for lower-cost contention access bus networks using less expensive coaxial cabling.

Coaxial cable—A cable with two conductors situated on a common axis.

Cochannel—A type of interference caused by the reception of a desired signal as well as a weaker reflected signal at the same frequency.

Combining network—A series of couplers or splitters (or equivalent circuits) used to combine RF energy and commonly used in headends to combine various signal inputs from modulators, signal processors, and other signal sources.

Crossmodulation—A form of distortion caused by the mixing of signals of different frequencies to produce subsidiary signals at sum and difference frequencies of the main frequencies.

CSMA/CD—Carrier sense multiple access with collision detection. A contention bus access method used on IEEE 802.3 and Ethernet LANs in which network devices wishing to transmit listen for other traffic and initiate transmissions if no other station is occupying the medium. Each station listens for collisions while transmitting; the station ceases transmission if a collision occurs. After a wait period, transmission is attempted again.

dBmV—A decibel referenced to 1 millivolt. dBmV is a method for measuring and describing an absolute signal level on a broadband network, in contrast to a dB, which describes the amount of change only.

Decibel (dB)—A measurement of signal level change that describes the amount of change but does not describe the actual signal level itself. It is a ratio of input power to output power.

Demodulation—The process of removing an RF carrier to read the baseband information it carriers.

Dielectric—A material used in coaxial cable to support the center conductor and insulate it.

Diplex filter—A low-pass and high-pass filter used to separate signals passing in the forward and reverse paths on a broadband network.

Directional coupler—A highly directional tapping device producing unequal output legs from a single input leg. It is used to tap RF energy off a cable or from an amplifier to feed distribution legs. Positioned 180° in reverse, a directional coupler acts as a combiner of signals.

Directional tap—A combination of directional coupler and one or more splitters to tap RF energy off a cable and feed it to several ports.

Directivity—A measurement of how well power is isolated between the tap port of a directional coupler and the output port of the same coupler.

Distortion—Any unwanted change in the desired shape of an RF waveform as it moves through amplifiers on a network.

Distribution system—In an larger sense, the entire system of amplifiers, cables, passive devices, and power supplies used to transport signals from the headend to user devices on a broadband network. Usually specifically refers to that portion of the cable plant starting at the bridger amplifiers and extending to all user ports.

Downstream—The forward path used by signals in a broadband system traveling from the headend to user ports.

Drop cable—RG-59 or RG-6 flexible cabling used to attach user devices to a wallplate.

Dual cable—A type of broadband network design using two different cables to carry outbound and inbound signals. Since all outbound signals are on one cable and all return signals on the other, no frequency translation system is required at the headend.

Egress—Leakage of energy on a broadband network into the atmosphere.

Equalizer—A circuit used to modify the frequency response of a group of frequencies to produce a flat response across the band.

FDDI—Fiber distributed data interface, a new proposed standard for token-passing ring topology, fiber optic LANs operating at 100 Mb/s.

Feedforward—An amplification technique that provides better distortion performance by phase inversion of the distortion components.

Field strength meter—A test instrument that measures signal level. Also known as a signal level meter.

Flat loss—Equal loss at all frequencies. Most passive devices and attenuators exhibit flat loss.

FM band—The range of frequencies between 88 and 108 MHz, used by over-the-air broadcasters for FM radio signals.

Frequency—The number of times per second that a signal oscillates between its high and low points.

Frequency modulation (FM)—A method for representing information by varying the frequency of a carrier wave.

Frequency response—Change in gain or loss of signal amplitude as frequency is varied across a passband.

Gain—A measure of signal amplitude increase, measured in decibels.

Gateway—Hardware and software used to connect two completely dissimilar LANs.

Gigahertz (GHz)—One billion cycles per second.

Guard band—A dedicated portion of a system's spectrum that is set aside to separate two adjacent frequency blocks or channels.

Harmonic—A subsidiary waveform produced at much reduced level at a multiple of a fundamental frequency.

Headend—The physical location as well as the equipment used at the base of a broadband system. Headend equipment can include satellite reception or transmission gear, antennas, preamplifiers, demodulators and modulators, signal processors, character generators and TV cameras, status monitoring computers and software, network management consoles, bridges, routers, and gateways.

Hertz (Hz)—A frequency rate of 1 cycle per second.

High band—The block of frequencies between TV channels 7 and 13, running from 174 to 216 MHz.

Hum modulation—A form of distortion caused by the interaction of ac power and RF signals.

IEEE—Institute of Electrical and Electronics Engineers, a major international standards-setting group and professional organization.

IEEE 802—A group of subcommittees working on LAN standards for the IEEE.

IEEE 802.2—Logical link control standard.

IEEE 802.3—Contention bus access protocol.

IEEE 802.4—Token-passing bus standard for broadband media. Currently the physical layer specification for the manufacturing automation protocol.

IEEE 802.5—Token-passing ring standard over twisted pair media. Currently the standard used by IBM for its token ring network.

IEEE 802.6—Metropolitan area network standards group.

IEEE 802.7—Standard for broadband LANs.

IEEE 802.8—Fiber optic LAN standards group.

Impedance—The total amount of opposition to the flow of a current through a device or cable. Impedance generally is frequency dependent.

Ingress—Leakage of off-air signal energy into a broadband plant.

Insertion loss—The difference in signal level between the input and output ports of any device on a broadband network.

Intermodulation—The mixing of two RF carriers that produces beat products that are sum products of the fundamental frequencies.

Internet—A layer of the open systems interconnection model known as the network layer.

Internetworking—The process of linking two or more LANs, either locally or over long distance.

Isolation—The degree of attenuation of RF signals between one of the output ports of a splitter or directional coupler and the other output port.

Kilohertz (kHz)—A thousand cycles per second.

LAN-WAN—The process of linking two or more local area networks at long distance over a wide area network of some kind.

Local area network (LAN)—A privately owned communications network operating at high speed over relatively small distances and linking computers, peripherals, and other devices.

Loop resistance—The dc resistance of cable expressed as ohms per thousand feet.

Manchester encoding—A method for representing positive binary information by a high-to-low signal level transition in the middle of a bit cell. Zero information is represented by a low-to-high transition.

Manufacturing automation protocol (MAP)—A standard for factory-automation LANs protomoting interoperability of equipment and software from differing vendors. Originally developed by General Motors and now spearheaded by the MAP/TOP Users Group of the Society of Manufacturing Engineers.

Mb/s—Megabits per second, a measure of data transmission speed.

Megahertz (MHz)—One million cycles per second.

Midband—The frequency spectrum between TV channels 6 and 7, running from 108 to 174 MHz.

Mini-MAP—A subset of the manufacturing automation protocol requiring use of physical and link layers only and allowing restricted communication between nodes on a single mini-MAP cable segment.

Modem—A contraction of modulator demodulator. A device used to combine baseband information with an analog carrier for transport over an analog transmission medium.

Modulation—The process of mixing a baseband signal with an RF carrier for transportation on an analog network.

Multidrop—A modem communication technique in which a single master modem polls subsidiary modems on a roll call basis. Sometimes referred to as *master-slave* technique.

Noise figure—The amount of noise generated by an electronic device that will be added to signals processed through it.

Nonreturn to zero (NRZ)—A form of coding in which logical ones are represented by a nonzero signal level while logical zeros are represented by defined zero levels.

Phase modulation—A form of modulation in which the phase of signal is inverted to represent a change of bit from logical one to logical zero, or *vice versa*.

Phase-shift keying (PSK)—A form of phase modulation using only a few discrete values to represent the phase shift.

Pilot carrier—A special carrier used to control AGC or ASC circuits in amplifiers.

Protocol—A set of rules and formats governing communications between devices.

Push-pull—An amplifier technique that provides better distortion and noise performance by using pairs of gain circuits to cancel second-order products.

Remodulator—A signal translation device similar to a translator in that it upconverts signals from one frequency range to a higher range. A remodulator strips off the inbound RF carriers before remodulating the outbound signals, however, and thus provides better noise performance than a translator.

Repeater—Hardware and software required to join two LAN segments using the same protocols but possibly different physical media. On a broadband LAN, repeaters are called amplifiers. Repeaters operate at the physical layer of the open systems interconnection (OSI) protocol suite.

Return loss—A measure of reflection that compares the level of the original wave with the level of the reflected wave.

Router—Hardware and software used to connect two LANs that have the same network architecture through the first three levels of the OSI model.

Second harmonic—A signal whose frequency is twice or one half the frequency of the main signal.

Second-order beat—An unwanted carrier created by the mixing of two RF carriers with each other.

Sideband—An analog waveform has a center frequency and two declining levels of energy on either side of the peak frequency. Each of these is called a sideband.

Signal-to-noise ratio (SNR)—A ratio comparing signal levels of baseband information to the level of noise contained by that signal.

Single-ended—An amplifier technology originally developed early in the history of cable TV that used a single transistor as the gain stage. It produced significant second-order products. It has been replaced by push-pull, parallel hybrid, and feedforward technologies.

Slope—The difference in amplifier gain, expressed in decibels, between the lowest and highest frequencies in the passband.

StarLAN—A standard for 1-MB/s CSMA/CD networks running on twisted pair wiring.

Status monitoring—Network control sytems that typically will show out-of-tolerance conditions for amplifiers and power supplies on a broadband network.

Sub-band—The frequency range from 5 to 54 MHz.

Superband—The range of frequencies between VHF channel 13 and UHF channel 14, running from 216 to 300 MHz.

System level—The level of the highest signal frequency in the passband at the output of each amplifier.

Tap—A device used to remove a portion of the RF energy from a coaxial cable.

Tap loss—The insertion loss of an RF signal from input to tap port.

TCP/IP—Transmission control protocol/internet protocol. A protocol suite developed by the Department of Defense and gaining popularity as a way of connecting diverse computing devices.

Technical and office protocols (TOP)—A companion standard to MAP and designed as the front office automation network.

10Base5—IEEE 802.3 standard for contention access coaxial cable LANs running on 50-Ω cabling at 10 Mb/s.

Terminator—A resistive device used to cap an unused cable and prevent reflections.

Tilt—A difference in signal level between the lowest and highest frequencies carried in a passband and produced by an amplifier circuit. Output from an amplifier sometimes is deliberately tilted to compensate for the slope of the cable segment that follows the amplifier.

Topology—The physical layout and architecture of a local area network. Common topologies are the bus, tree, star, and ring. Wide area networks use a mesh topology.

Translator—A device at a headend that converts a block of inbound frequencies from one range to another for retransmission outbound from the headend.

Triple beat—A third-order beat created by the mixing of three separate carriers.

Twisted pair—Common telephone-type wiring consisting of strands of copper wire twisted around each other.

UHF—The ultra high frequency band runs from 470 to 806 MHz and is rarely used on broadband networks.

Upstream—Signals traveling from network ports toward the headend are moving upstream. Sometimes this is referred to as return or reverse path.

Vestigial sideband—Bandwidth can be conserved by recovering all the signal information from a sine wave by using a single sideband rather than both sidebands. Vestigial sideband transmission supresses one of the sidebands.

VHF—Very high frequencies are those between 30 and 300 MHz.

Wide area network—A communications network operating over long distance, such as AT&T, MCI, Sprint, or SBS.

Wiring closet—A room or other location at a facility where network wiring is concentrated for attachment to devices. Wiring closets sometimes are used as repeater or hub sites.

INDEX